Mary Elizabeth Moragne Davis

Lays from the Sunny Lands

Mary Elizabeth Moragne Davis

Lays from the Sunny Lands

ISBN/EAN: 9783744710985

Printed in Europe, USA, Canada, Australia, Japan

Cover: Foto ©Thomas Meinert / pixelio.de

More available books at **www.hansebooks.com**

LAYS

FROM THE

SUNNY LANDS.

BY

MRS. MARY E. MORAGNÉ DAVIS,

Author of the "British Partisan," "Rencontre," and other pieces in prose and verse.

"Though Time thy bloom is stealing,
There's still beyond his art
The wild flower wreath of feeling,—
The sunshine of the heart."
—*Halleck.*

BUFFALO:
MOULTON, WENBORNE AND COMPANY.

1888.

Dedication.

TO the surviving friends, whose warm appreciation of my earlier efforts in literature has been my inspiration and strengthener in later studies: To the children and grandchildren, whom they have taught to love and honor my name and character: To all admirers of the beautiful, wherever found, this little volume is most lovingly inscribed by

THE AUTHOR.

TALLEDEGA, ALA., 1888.

CONTENTS.

	PAGE.
ÆSTHETICS,	1
A HOME IN THE SOUTH,	3
PICKING UP THE CRUMBS,	6
THE MARRIAGE OF CUPID AND PSYCHE,	8
THE MOCKING BIRD,	11
THE LEGEND OF ST. ARNULPH,	13
TO CARRIE,	15
BYE AND BYE,	16
THE LILY OF THE VALE,	19
LINES TO THE SAVANNAH RIVER,	20
IN MEMORIAM,	22
AN EVENING WALK IN AUTUMN,	24
HOME MEMORIES,	26
LAST WORDS OF JAMES HENLEY THORNWELL, D. D.,	29
HE DOETH ALL THINGS WELL,	32
NOTHING TO DO,	34
THE LOST ROSEBUD,	36
THE WOODS,	38
THE LADY OF THE HILL,	40
ELEGY,	42
GO FORWARD,	45
THE MILLER AND THE CAMEL,	48
THE RANCHERO'S CHILD,	51
SUNSET AMONG THE MOUNTAINS,	54
MY SISTERS,	56
LINES FOR THE ALBUM OF A YOUNG FRIEND,	58
THE HUGUENOT'S FAREWELL,	60
AFTER THE BATTLE,	63
THE WHITE CROSS LEAGUE,	66
LES BELLES AMITIÉS,	67
UNFORGOTTEN THINGS,	72

CONTENTS.

	PAGE.
THE GLORY AND THE GRIEF,	75
LINES TO A MAGNOLIA BUD,	77
THE BABY,	79
THE BOTANIC RAMBLE,	81
THE VILLAGE CHURCH BELL,	85
CONSIDER THE LILIES,	87
JACOB AT THE WELL,	89
BESIDE THE SYRIAN WELL,	92
TALLULAH,	94
ALGÆ,	100
SCENE ON THE HUDSON,	103
WASHINGTON IRVING,	105
OUT OF THE DEPTHS,	107
LINES OCCASIONED BY A FROST IN APRIL,	109
SONG,	110
OUR BOY HEROES,	112
WARFARE,	115
LITTLE COTTAGE HOME,	118
SHADOWS,	119
LOVE AND THE FLOWERS,	124
MY FOREST HOME,	126
POOR LITTLE ZIP,	128
THE OLD HOMESTEAD,	133
THE PIONEER,	139
POOR RACHEL,	144
OLD GEOFFREY,	148
THE BROKEN HEART,	153
THE IGNIS FATUUS, OR GONDEMA AND FABRICIO,	157

LAYS FROM THE SUNNY LANDS

LAYS FROM THE SUNNY LANDS.

ÆSTHETICS.

The blizzard was past, old Eurus came
Whetting his scimeter after the rain.

He pierced the mist on the Mountain's side
And flung it in crystals far and wide.

Each china-berry an ear-drop wore;
And the mosses wept jewels from every spore.

The cedars bore, on their finger tips
Goblets, just fitted to fairy lips.

Down in the valley, the rifted trees
Like minarets stood, in the stiffening breeze.

The Mountain, in robes of silver grey,
Looked like a Mussulman, knelt to pray.

Drinking the breath of the icy morn
At the open window, I stood forlorn;

But the stillness, and awe of that glory, dim,
Was inditing for me a choral hymn;

When little Marie, with thoughtful brow
Ran in, to question the why? and how?

" See grandmamma, this spire of grass
　How beautiful 'tis, in its house of glass!"

" Yes, all His works are bright and good,
　My darling child, if we understood.

" The mist imprisoned the feathery tines;
　And the chill air wove it, in crystal lines.

" 'Tis thus in nature, we always find
　Marks of a loving, grand design,

" But see, on the window pane, how soon
　The vapors their native garb resume.

" Sweet Zephyrus' wings are fluttering round,
　And the pearly frost-work is sliding down.

" The atoms are free to move again;
　Distilling a noiseless, gentle rain.

" There are hopes, dear child, which as brightly gleam
　That dissolve into mist, like this fairy dream;

" And we learn, from the atmosphere's fitful play,
　That the most beautiful visions will pass away."

A HOME IN THE SOUTH.

They tell me of homes, in the cold, icy North,
    Where beauty with splendor vies,
Where genius and culture have plighted their troth
    To dazzle and charm the eyes;
But I have a cot by the streamlet's side,
With a verdant Savanna opening wide,
Where the honey-bee revels in beds of thyme,
And cow-bells tinkle a drowsy chime,
    And this is the home for me!
A home in the South, the sweet, sunny South,
    A home in the South for me!

They whisper of vales in the far distant West
    Which the wonders of Nature show;
There's a snowy wreath on the mountain crest
    While summer is ripe below;
But I have a heaven of turquoise blue
Where the liquid stars seem melting through,
And all night long in the moon's pale sheen
The mocking bird sings to his fairy queen;—
    Oh, a home in the South for me!
A home in the South, the beautiful South,
    A home in the South for me!

I envy not old England's halls,
    Nor the pride of her hedges green,
'Though the nightingale's song so bewitchingly falls
    The note of the cuckoo between.
There's a sweet, low trill at fall of eve
Quivering along through the cool, green leaves;

And my red-winged starling's harshest notes
Are sweeter to me than those foreign throats; —
  Oh, a home in the South for me!
A home in the South, the sweet-voiced South,
  A home in the South for me!

Italia's skies are fair, I ween,
  And the flush of her purple grapes;
Her marble halls, with sculptures gleam,
  And she has relics of wondrous shapes;
But the glittering leaves of the jessamine vine
Around my cottage verandas twine,
And dearer are they, than those ruins gray,
While under its blossoms my children play; —
  Oh, a home in the South for me!
A home in the South, my own bright South,
  A home in the South for me!

Oh, give me a home 'neath the evergreen bowers
  Where the oriole's palace swings;
And in, and out, 'mong the orange flowers
  Gleam the tints of his golden wings;
Where fairy hands with the long moss play,
Through varnished green, and with weird gray,
And the sand-fly whistles his treble stave,
And the cayman bellows beneath the wave; —
  Oh, a home in the South for me!
A home in the South, the dreamy South,
  A home in the South for me!

Yes, give me a home, free from anarchy's rule,
  And suspicion's murky tread;
From the pedant's scorn, and the bigot's school,
  And "isms" of every head,
Where shoulder to shoulder, we stand and fight

For honor and virtue, for truth and right;
Where each man's face is an open glass,
Where thoughts are mirrored to all that pass:
  Oh, this is the home for me! —
A home in the South, in the grand old South,
  A home in the South for me!

PICKING UP THE CRUMBS.

The winter sky was clouded o'er, and dull,
The wintry wind blew piercingly and cold;
And as I shook my cloth upon the snow
A little bird came hopping to the door
      Picking up the crumbs.

Some little children, seated on the floor
Were playing with their spoons, and casting o'er
Each other morsels of their dainty bread;
A little greedy dog with shaggy head,
      Was picking up the crumbs.

A farmer boy, beside the water's edge
Eating his lunch upon the broomy sedge
Let fall some fragments on the limpid stream;
The little fishes in and out did gleam,
      Picking up the crumbs.

A little, willful child, with angry frown
Threw out his " bon bon " on the grassy ground;
Not very long I chanced that way to stray,—
The busy ants had moved it all away
      Picking up the crumbs.

And this, I said, is silent Nature's rede
To teach us, if we wisefully would heed,
That littles and by littles make a heap;—
That many creatures do their being keep
      Picking up the crumbs.

PICKING UP THE CRUMBS.

The Saviour would himself a lesson give
That nothing should be lost on which we live;
When the great feast of miracles was stayed,
Twelve fragmentary basketfuls were made
     Picking up the crumbs.

Just so with scraps of wisdom, which we find
In books, or in tradition, if we mind
To catch them, as we journey on in haste,
A loaf of knowledge we'll obtain at last
     Picking up the crumbs.

Time ever dropping,— as they swiftly turn,—
His golden sands into the gloomy urn
Reminds us, that these precious gems are ours,
And we may cumulate the work of years
     Picking up the crumbs.

All Nature's great developments are made
From microscopic atoms. Forms and shades
And tints, and colorings, and voices train
The taste of man. Perfection he must gain
     Picking up the crumbs.

The God who sees a sparrow when it falls,
And numbers e'en our hairs, has set o'er all
A providence minute, and he receives
The highest meed who most attention gives,
     To picking up the crumbs.

THE MARRIAGE OF CUPID AND PSYCHE.

'TIS very clear
The ancients in their theories, came near
　The truth divine, 'though in their practice, far
From doing justice to a thing so dear,—
　Domestic love, sweetest, beyond compare
Of all things here — they would not need to sense,
Nor make the slave of self, nor dupe of folly; hence
The youthful god of Love — as we are told —
They married to sweet Psyche, or the soul!

　　Thus are we taught
That not in silken chains of pleasure caught,
　Nor won by golden bribes, should Cupid be;
But by the sweeter harmonies of thought,
　Tuning to one refrain, the minstrelsy
Of holy love, whose highest key-note is
In moral beauty, and in mental bliss.
Only a spiritual communion, gives
That blessed trust, which in this tableau lives.

　　Standing there,
The most illustrious, and loveliest pair
　Of wedded hearts, among the forms divine,
What grace and beauty in their eyes appear!
　What dignity in all their actions shine,
Sweetly transmitting down to after years,
A model image of that Love, which bears
Under the marriage yoke, an equal share
In all the fond concerns of joy or care!

Wingéd are both,
Which signifies to us, that nothing loath,
   They fly, with speed, at Love's inviting call —
With such alacrity, on each side, doth
   Support and cheer — anticipating all
Wishes before expressed; — want cannot come
Within the precinct of their sheltered home
While rising each, on Love's unwearied wing
They soar above the cares that life may bring.

Veiléd they show,
That Love its charm to Modesty doth owe
   Who ever stands, fair maiden, by their side
Speaking soft words and pure;
   And putting down the arrogance of pride,
Which makes its claim, superior, to be seen
With coarser jest and ribaldry, this I ween
Would drive the tender passion from the breast
And entertain instead, a bare-faced guest.

Hymen goes before
Bearing a lighted torch, whose glow
   Shall guide them all the way,
And warm them more and more
   With pure devotion 'till their heads be gray.
He leads them by a chain,
Entwined about them, o'er and o'er again;
Binding them fast, in one continuous bond,
A Gordian knot, but equable and fond.

This chain is not
From brass, nor yet from iron heavy wrought,
   For marriage should not be a thraldom high,
Nor like the slave, into the shambles brought
   In durance vile, should either sigh;

And neither is it made of links of gold,
Within whose meshes hearts are bought and sold;
But 'tis of pearls, most exquisitely fair,
Unstained with selfishness, and light to wear.

    Sweet Psyche and her love,
Caressingly, between them, held a dove,
 To signify, that like that faithful bird
Each from the other, never more shall rove;
 But ever true, in thought, in deed, in word,
E'en in the topmost boughs of duty sing;
Filling all life with cooings of the spring;
Keeping the ear still open to that call,
Which first, its raptured senses did enthrall.

    Lastly, with feathers curled,
And wings all shrivelled, and closely furled,
 A gentle genius, seems to intimate
That through the varied world
 Neither must wish to find another mate;
But as his wings are now unfit for flight
So must they linger near him with delight;
And as with Love began their blest career,
So, still with Love must end this union dear.

THE MOCKING BIRD.

Bird of the South! Imperial prince of song,
That through the lone hours lovest to prolong
The tidal wave of music dear to me!
A debt of gratitude I owe to thee,
Who soothed with melody the throbs of pain,
Through the night watches, till the morning came.
Perched on the leafy hedges, far away,
Pouring thy soul out to the moon's pale ray,
Or, 'neath my window, in the garden bowers,
Where sits thy duteous mate, enshrined in flowers,
The fond Epithalamium thou dost sing,
Both night and day, will tears and laughter bring.

Bird of the South! they do thee willful wrong,
Who say thou art a plagiarist in song;
And I, thy grateful service will repay
By proving thee an artist in thy way,
In the alembic of thy little throat
Distilling sweetest strains from every note
Which Nature to the choral tribes hath given,
Thus echoing, in full, the voice of heaven!
Thou doest what all amateurs have done,
Trilling the chords of harmony begun,
In shakes, arpeggios, and "winding bout"
Of labyrinthine sweetness "long drawn out."

Bird of the South! so mocked art thou, then,
Though from the lark, the red-bird, and the wren
Thou drawest the themes thou dost so sweetly sing.
Of all composers, thou the very king!
Calling each beauty from the feathered throng
To weave into thy microcosm of song;

Stringing with endless wit, the chain of sound,
Where pearls and golden links of tone abound,
Where "L'Allegro" "Il Penseroso" meet.
Richly diverse, yet joined in cadence sweet.
No hypercriticism can it be,
Sweet caroler, that thus entranceth thee!
  Bird of the South! Bird of the sunny lands!
Around thee, every social thought expands,
Of home, and flowers, and breezy woodlands, too;
Thou makest e'en sorrow brighter to the view!
Partner in all my joys, solace in misery,
A loving compact I have formed with thee.
But more, sweet friend, I love thee as the type
Of Southern beauty, which no wrongs can wipe
From my heart or thine. Oppression cannot bring
Blight on its hues, nor any discord fling
In thy patrician lay. For me and thee,
  Bird of the Sunny South, there can no exile be.

THE LEGEND OF ST. ARNULPH.

How surely God has written on the heart
His philanthropic lessons, all apart
From Superstition's rule, or bigot's art!

The prepossession through the nations ran
Inscribed on legends culled from every land
Connecting love to God with love to man.

St. Arnulph, a physician's son, was reared,
And him his sire had with care prepared
To share the "Healer's" high and great award.

St. Arnulph to his father said, one day:
"Let me into the cloister go, I pray;
To serve our God is far the better way."

"'Tis true, my son," the father said, "but then,
As a physician you may serve Him, when
You also try to serve your fellow-men.

"But go into thy closet now and pray,
Thy anxious quest before thy Maker lay;—
To-morrow I will do as thou shalt say."

The pious Arnulph to his closet went,
And asked of God, as near the throne he bent;—
His days might all be in His service spent.

And lo! an angel stood within the room
His right hand filled with roses, in their bloom
Shedding on all around a rich perfume.

The angelic messenger looked up and smiled.
"Behold," said he, "the offerings, my child,
Of those, no longer by their sins beguiled!"

"But in thy left hand also," Arnulph said,
"I see another wreath of roses red;
And wherefore is their grateful odor fled?"

"These are *thy* offerings Arnulph; these alone
The gifts thou broughtest to God, their sweetness flown,
Because thy heart is very selfish grown.

"For know, the fragrant gifts of my right hand
Embalmed in *love* have been; so understand
He serves God best who serves his fellow-man!"

TO CARRIE.

(*In an Album.*)

My gentle friend, upon thy brow
   No shadows from the future play;
But living on the joyous now
   Thy spirit must be,— will be gay.

And could the sunny days of youth
   Live on in one eternal spring,
Could earth become the home of truth
   I'd love to see thee laugh and sing.

But even o'er those vernal hours
   Life's murky shadows often fall,
And tho' we grasp some fleeting flowers,
   The serpent's trail is over all.

They who that mission would fulfill
   Which to the loving heart is given,
Must weep with those that weep, and still
   Look up in patient trust to heaven.

They who that holy path would find
   Where fraud and malice have not been,
Must seek it where life's sorrows end,
   And where the joys of heaven begin.

Then hope not for perennial smiles
   To brighten up this earth with love;
The amaranth flower can only bloom
   In the sweet paradise above.

BYE AND BYE.

" Man never is but always to be blest."

Somewhere adown the stream of time,
Floating along in haste sublime,
Lies a land, never seen by mortal eye;
'Tis a sweet little island called " Bye and Bye."

It may be about us; or it may be afar,
Cradled beneath the evening star;
Or Eternity's sands may be drifting high
On that mystical land of the sweet " Bye and Bye."

But brilliant fancies around it play;
And happiness there never cloys, they say;
And riches that Crœsus could not buy
Fill the dear little island, " Bye and Bye."

Oh, this beautiful island! weary and worn
We wander, darkling through paths unknown;
But hope ever points to a beacon high
Where we catch the sunshine of " Bye and Bye."

The laborer, as he sows the ground,
Watching and toiling the whole year round,
Sees rest and comfort drawing nigh,
With his garnered sheaves, in the " Bye and Bye."

The merchant, too, as day by day
Small gains his weary vigils pay,
Dreams nightly of his Argosie
Laden with wealth in the " Bye and Bye."

The soldier, through his griefs untold,
Tired and hungry, wet and cold,
Hears "Glory," with her trumpet high,
Sound "Pæans" in the "Bye and Bye."

See that fond mother bending there,
Smiling, but faint with cradle-care,
She whispers soft, as her fingers fly,
"These babes shall comfort me 'Bye and Bye.'"

The boy grows up, erect and tall,
And, looking away from top and ball,
Sees manhood's brightest honors lie
In the glorious land of the "Bye and Bye."

To the maiden fair all nature seems
A 'wilderment of golden dreams;
But their sweetest development waits, to try
This fairy island, "Bye and Bye."

The Christian wades through troubled seas,
He asks not for pleasure, he seeks not ease;
But he points to a vision beyond the sky —
His mansion of rest in the "Bye and Bye."

Oh, this beautiful island! it leads us on
Under the banner the Saviour won,
To strive for the crown which faith can descry
Awaiting the just, in the "Bye and Bye."

Oh, this beautiful island! The tempter lures
The minds of his subjects this spot to choose
For the place of repentance, and so belie
The promises sweet of the "Bye and Bye"

Oh, the promises sweet of that blissful shore!
Where hearts once united shall part no more;
Where all at the Saviour's feet shall lie,
In the beautiful halls of the "Bye and Bye."

THE LILY OF THE VALE.

WHEN, bending to the passing gale
Thy slender stem, and cheek so pale,
Thy soft breath scents the dewy vale,
    Sweet lily! — then,
When stooping o'er the water's side,
Though brightly imaged in its tide,
Thy modest chalice knows no pride
    Nor jealous pain.

On thee should rambling school boy light,
Attracted by thy petals bright,
A broken stem would mark his flight
    In thoughtless haste.
But, envious is thy fate, sweet flower,
Secluded in thy sylvan bower,
Apart from sad temptation's power,
    And ruthless waste.

Thou art the soul of thoughts refined,
The image of a spotless mind,
Where delicacy sits enshrined,
    Thou peerless one!
And gentle maidens, pure and true,
May learn from thee, that not to woo
Will make them sweeter to the view,
    And scorned by none.

LINES TO THE SAVANNAH RIVER.

GENTLE river, gentle river,
   Softly as thy surges roll,
Flow the thoughts which thou awakest
   On my idealistic soul;—
Rolling on from childhood's haven
   Thou hast treasured dreams of mine,
Till the slightest breath that stirs thee,
Wakes a murmuring of "Lang Syne."

River, I have marked thy current
   Gliding from its mountain springs,
Leaping in its foaming eddies,
   Flashing on its silver wings;
Yet to me, thy stream is fairest
   Where thou spreadest still and wide,
Blending such resistless beauty,
   With the grandeur of thy tide.

River, gentle river, tell me,
   Is there aught of mystic spell,
Mermaid's haunt, or Nereid's grotto,
   Garnered in thy crystal well?
Oft when lying, idly musing,
   In some still, sequestered nook
Was it sprite, or wandering zephyr
   Flowery petals on me shook?

Haply, spirits long departed
   Roam along this fragrant shore,
Lingering in the spell, which binds them
   To the haunts they loved of yore;

Oft, when sporting on thy bosom
  In a shallop, lightly bound,
I have fancied, Elfin music
  Trembled in the waters round.

Haply, here, the Indian maiden
  Wafted in her light canoe
To the dipping oar makes rhythm
  With the songs of "long ago";
Haply, here, the quivered chieftain,
  Floating down thy glassy tide,
Sings the war-songs of his nation
  To entrance his dusky bride.

River, many a barque has tried thee,
  Many a foot has pressed thy shore;
But a *race* has vanished from thee
  Thou shalt never gladden more.
River,— thou enduring river!
  Many ages yet to come;
Though *another* race has perished
  Thou wilt brightly sparkle on!

IN MEMORIAM.

MISS M. C. CALHOUN, OF SOUTH CAROLINA, AUTHOR OF "KEOWEE WALTRES."

We know that the spirit, on earth leaves a trace
    Of the feelings, which prove it divine;
As roses, tho' withered, still hallow the vase
    Where they, in their freshness, reclined;—
As the breathings of music remain in the shell,
    When the soul of the minstrel is fled;
And float on the breeze, in harmonious swell
    When we waken the chords of the dead.

We know, that the heart, in its hungering, craves
    Some token, its thoughts to recall;—
For thee seemed enough the proud banner that waves
    In the light of thy ancestral hall;
But the spirit of poesy breathed on thy soul;
    And Keowee's legends around,
Awoke all the echoes of harmonies, old,
    And attuned them to metrical sound.

We know not, if beauty thy person adorned;
    But we know, there was beauty of soul
On "Etowa's" soft liquid measure 'tis borne;
    On "Toxawa's" wild waves it rolls.
Oh, some on ambition's fierce tempest are tost;
    And some are by vanity moved;—
For thee it is sweet,— who so early was lost,—
    Thus to sing, in the hearts thou has loved?

We trust thou art gone to some island of rest,
   Where music and rapture are one,
Where the soul never feels that enchanting distress
   Which thrills in thy sorrow-fraught tones.
They wail for thee!— wail for thee! swan of the South;
   And we, the sweet death notes prolong;
Oh! who would not lay down the chaplet in youth,
   To be thus embalméd in song!

AN EVENING WALK IN AUTUMN.

Oh, how sweet and how cheering
   In solitude to roam,
When the pale tints of evening
   Diffuse a soft gloom.

When the song birds have fled
   To their nightly repose;
And the broad disk of Sol is o'erspread
   With opal and rose!

Oh, 'tis bliss to elope
   From the cares of the day;
At this hour, and in widest scope
   Nature around survey.

The plain, plodding rustic, list!
   Whistling as homeward he hies;
His plump cheek, how nut-brown it is!
   What joy in his quick, flashing eyes!

Adown the valley you gaze
   Where the steps of the Frost King are seen,
The woodside is one attaching maze,
   Purple, and gold, and green.

'Mid rustling leaves, — hist! the squirrel steals
   Belated to his store;
And the whirring wing of the partridge, wheels
   To seek her mate once more.

Through the russet wood, remote from sight
    As far as the eye extends;
Where Dame Nature exhibits her naked plight,
    A solemn calm impends.

Lo! on the crest of the high-peaked pine
    A sudden glory shines!
There the last beams of Sol recline
    In shimmering broken lines.

High in the west one radiant pearl
    Emerges to the sight; —
Venus, thou goddess of yore! unfurl
    Thy charms to the soft twilight!

And mark in the east, that rising sphere,
    Peerless in majesty!
How grand her strides! her beams how clear,
    As she walks o'er the turquoise sea!

Oh, hast roamed at even, when moonbeams shone
    And the glittering stars were at play, —
To heaven, thy sorrows hast thou bemoaned
    Till thy cares have died away?

'Tis ecstasy! — this sense divine
    Of the *glorious things that be*,
It ennobles thought, it lifts the mind
    To musings heavenly!

Found among the papers of my brother.—W. C. M.

HOME MEMORIES.

They played together, 'neath the shades
  Which girt their forest home;
They sported in the sunny glades
  Or on the hillsides roamed; —
So full of life and childish glee,
So fond, in their young purity
You would have deemed, the world could ne'er
Have separated things so dear.

They grew together, — side by side, —
  Till childhood's glee was gone;
And youth had won its brow of pride,
  Its eye and lip of song;
The same in love, in heart, and life,
As free from stain, as far from strife,
It was a pleasant sight to see
These children of one family!

How little recked they of the pain
  Which coming years might bring!
From care and sorrow's gloomy train
  That home had bounded in, —
Alas! for tears that all must shed,
Both for the living and the dead!
There's many a footstep silent now,
Which gladdened that sweet home of yore.

She faded with the autumn leaf,
  A sweet and modest girl;

Her life had been as fair as brief,
   Too gentle for this world;
Like some sweet flower, o'er which has passed
The rushing of the deadly blast,
Scattered in freshness on the ground,
She sank in beauty to the tomb!

One perished in a foreign land;—
   A brave and noble boy;
The brightest of that happy band,
   The merriest in his joy.
The duty to his country owed
He placed above all cherished good;
And poured his life's blood on the soil
He won with so much pain and toil.

And one, the pride and hope of all,
   Upon the world is cast;
Bound to Ambition's stormy barque,
   Yet weary of the past.
The traveler of many lands
The soldier, scholar, patriot stands;
But often does he crave the shade
Where in his infancy he played.

Another, lured by love away,
   Hath made herself a nest;
And where her little fledgelings play
   There she delights to rest.
Ambition's wings are folded down;
And vain desires and hopes are gone;
Yet many a yearning thought she sends
To the old home and childhood friends!

Another yet,—most firm of soul,
   Hath gained himself a place.

By energy and stern control.
　　A blessing to his race;
Yet not alone; a gentle friend
Doth to his cottage beauty lend;
And infant greetings well atone
For voices of his native home.

Such is the various fate of some
　　Who at one board were fed;
Three to their several tasks are gone;
　　And two are with the dead!
Around the parent tree still cling
Some branches of the later spring;
But changed, as by a wizard's spell,
Is the dear home we loved so well.

Still proudly wave those fine old trees;
　　But seldom there is heard
Glad music rushing on the breeze,
　　By joy's wild fingers stirred;—
Upon each fair and youthful face
Lingers a sad and silent grace,
As if some cloud of days gone by
Were shadowing o'er their summer sky.

THE LAST WORDS OF JAMES HENLEY THORNWELL, D. D.

The seer lay meekly on his dying bed;
Unconscious of its woes. No plaint was there; but,
    gentle smiles instead
Played round his lips, and thrilled with holy fear
The looker's on,— because of angels near.

The conflict had been sharp. His raven hair
Bedewed with death's cold drops lay darkly there;
And in his eye was quenched the fire, sublime,
So lately in its intellectual prime.

The partner of his soul! Oh, who can tell
The sorrow which to her that hour befell!
And children dear who grew beneath his wing,
But now bereft of that safe sheltering!

And others, too, within that room of woe
Were weeping as they seldom wept before;
Because a sun was going down at noon;—
Because that tongue was paralyzed so soon!

Well might we here anticipate the wail
Of grief which borne on many a Southern gale
Filled every heart and echoed from each shore:
"The people's own— our Thornwell is no more!"

His Country's boast, the Church's hope and pride;
The book in which all Querists could confide;

The Orator, Logician, Patriot, Sage;
The man of men,—the greatest of his age!

But worth and fame redeem not! Here he lies
With pallid brow and closely veiléd eyes.
Behind he leaves a track of light divine;
But now he dies, and dying, leaves no sign.

What need of further proof? His life had been
An open conflict with the man of sin,
And all the trophies of his brilliant mind
Had humbly to his Saviour been resigned.

What need? what need? when daily o'er and o'er
He witness to the Christian's graces bore;
And from the dewy morning of his youth
Had laid his off'rings on the shrine of "Truth"!

No sounds now reach him from a world of grief,
But lo! he speaks in accents clear and brief;
While light from other worlds like sunset waves
With flick'ring shadows every feature laves.

At this last stage the great Physician came;
And touched his weary eyes with healing balm.
Christ would not leave his servant to go down
The dreary vale without some light around.

The curtain of the future was withdrawn,
And on his parting spirit gleamed the dawn,
The beautiful invisible! the blest
Fair mansions, where the weary rest.

"Wonderful!" "Beautiful!" they hear him say,
Surprise and rapture mingling in their play —

"Nothing but space;"—breaks on his joyous sense,
Again he softly cries, "Expanse! Expanse! Expanse!"

If thus the glorious shadowings alone,
Across the cold dark stream of Jordan shone,
What must the beatific vision be,
When on him burst the bright reality!

When through the happy realms of ambient space
His shackles dropt, he took his flight in haste,
And passed the bounds of many a rolling star,
Which scientists had looked on from afar!

When on the sapphire floor of heaven he trod,
And worshipped in the glorious court of God,
And saw the Lamb upon his jeweled throne,
And saw the Elders cast their glittering crowns.

Oh blessed man!—and blessed, blessed fate,
To find an open entrance at the gate
Where many knock, and knock, alas! in vain,
Departing thence, to dwell in endless pain.

HE DOETH ALL THINGS WELL.

"All things"? Dear Lord, sin boldly stalks around,
  Injustice reigns, oppressive acts abound,
  Deceit and violence usurp the earth
  And mock at innocence and modest worth.
"Man sees in part. The evil I allow
  Will only make my saints the fairer grow."

"All things"? And yet the proud oppress the poor,
  The good are beggars at the rich man's door,
  Power and wealth are given alike to few,
  The righteous seldom have the means to do.
"Power and wealth are dangerous foes to grace;
  I use them only in their proper place."

"All things"? Our fairest flowers are hedged with thorns,
  Mildew and blight spring ever in our corn;
  O'er all our brightest hopes a shadow falls,
  And every pleasure on the spirit palls.
"If on a bed of roses thou didst lie
  No words of mine could win thee to the sky."

"All things"! Thou mighty one! Floods waste and kill,
  The stormy winds fulfill thy direful will;
  Earthquake and pestilence, and fire and sword
  Harass us in our beautiful abode.
"Rebellious children must be taught to fear
  A God of glory and of vengeance near."

"All things"? My dearest Lord behold me now,
  What bitter writhings on my anguished brow!

HE DOETH ALL THINGS WELL.

The beauty of my life, my joy, my rest,
Thou takest away, and leavest me unblest.
"In no way could I wean thee from the world,
Unless thy idols from their throne I hurled."

"All things! all things"! My Father I am pressed
With anxious cares, by sharpest want distressed;
Through the deep gloom I see no pitying hand
Stretched over the dark gulf on which I stand.
"'Tis well, my child; thou wouldst not lean on me
Till all thy props had failed thee utterly."

"All things"? Under thy chastening hand I long have
    been
A weary sufferer, and thou hast seen
My spirit struggling with despair and grief
Because my term of service is so brief.
"Be still; it is thy Father's hand of love
Removing thee from all these ills above."

"He doeth all things well"! In wrath or love
The greatest good to all, his actings prove.
Nature and providence concurrent show
That truth and wisdom which no failure know.
Earth speaks in mysteries, but heaven shall tell
Through all her sounding aisles, "He doeth all things
    well."

NOTHING TO DO.

Nothing to do! And the world is full
   Of want, and care, and crime;
That law will you dare disannul
   Which maketh work divine?

Your heart is a garden, well I know,
   O'errun with noisome weeds;
Plough up the fallow ground and sow
   The soil with choicest seeds.

But let your work for *other's* weal,
   Not for your *own*, abound;
The truest guerdon of human zeal
   In self is never found.

Have you a mother bending down
   'Neath the sheaves of toil and grief?
Your young arm round her strongly wound
   Will sweetly bring relief.

You have a father, perchance, whose life
   Has been one thought for you;
Oh! have you nothing,— to soothe the strife
   Of age and care,— to do?

Your brothers,— Oh, how much they need
   Your hand to lead above!
No words against temptations plead
   So strong as a sister's love!

And if you have no flock to tend
   Go work in the common fold;
One wandering lamb, if you gather in,
   Then you have saved a soul!

The world is a field of duty, made
   To work in if you would;
"The poor ye always have," He said;
   And ye may do them good.

But if you can find no work, then pray
   The Lord of the "Harvest Home"
To bear you from fruitless days away
   Lest you become a drone.

THE LOST ROSEBUD.

Within our rural garden
  While summer smiled serene,
There grew six gentle rosebuds,
  Upon one parent stem.
By dews and showers nurtured
  And guarded with much care
They opened in the sunbeams,
  And promised passing fair.

But though to outward seeming
  This cluster bloomed so fair
A worm, within its bosom,
  Was darkly preying there.
Yet, was its work unheeded
  By the fond ones at her side,
Till the sweetest of the rosebuds
  Had drooped its head and died.

Then rose a wail of anguish
  From out that sister band
For the lost and lovely rosebud
  Which by their side did stand;
Nor ceased their vain lamentings,
  Though faith could point above
To a seraph-spirit blooming
  In imperishable love.

How did our mother languish
  For that pure and guileless breast

THE LOST ROSEBUD.

Which in the lonely churchyard
   We gently laid to rest;
She missed the kindly footsteps
   That came at her command,
She pined, amid her household,
   To see a broken band.

But now, to soothe that anguish,
   Sweet sister, thou art come
In lieu of that fair rosebud
   Which God has taken home.
Thou hast come with gentle goodness,
   Thou hast come with graces sweet,
And though there's one in heaven
   Our cluster's still complete!

THE WOODS.

"The country — the country wins me still."

The woods! The bright, the joyous woods!
Where birds and bees make concert good,
With croaking frogs, and insect wings
And many other gleesome things!
The babbling brooklet's noisy swell,
The violets, in the mossy dell,
The glen-side, with its wreaths of fern,
And nuts and berries in their turn
Bring back my childhood joys to me:
And then three merry boys I see,
Whose memory, — alas! is all
A sister's love may now recall,
Who shared with me the round-de-lay,
Dame Nature sung for us, each day.

The beautiful, the breezy wood!
Where in my early maidenhood
A happy, thoughtful girl I strayed
Through many a leafy copse and glade:
Or musing, on the greensward lay,
The greensward, rich with flow'rets gay:
And by my side was one, as fair
As wood-nymphs, or as Nereids are.
We sweet communion held of soul,
And conversed with the bards of old,
Under the spreading beech-tree's shade,
Or bowers, by thick "Bignonias" made,
With feathery arches overhead,

With crimson bells the floor o'erspread.
Ofttimes upon the river's brink
We stooped to see the snowdrops drink.
Ah me! how many years I've seen,
Since she through Beulah's land has been!

The woods! the grand old glorious woods,
Lifting their heads beyond the floods,
And whispering back the tales of eld
From sighing boughs — the tales that held
Our sires in such a wondrous awe
Of Nature's great unchanging law.
A mystery, sublime and wild;
I felt it when I was a child,
It thrilled me, when a woman grown;
I heard the wind's low, plaintive moan,
O'er *peace destroyed*, I feel it now,—
When time is silvering o'er my brow.

The strong, the free, the dauntless wood,
Which fire and flood and storm withstood
Through æons past, and still as blest
Come forth in the same gala dress!
Though shadows in my sunshine play
Thy garb is just as green and gay;
Though echoing sadly my regret
Thy voice is soft and soothing yet!
Here every bird is free to sing;
Here every bitter care takes wing,
And envy loses half its sting;
Here anger waxes cold and wan,
And silent thought has power to charm;
Here we may rest life's weary load,
And hold communion sweet with God.

THE LADY OF THE HILL.

In the rear of our dwelling, where the pine trees sped away;
When the mellow twilight deepened, and the stars were out at play,
Came a voice in mocking syllables, both musical and sweet,
The shouts of merry children, responsively to greet.

Above the sighing forest leaves the sportsman ofttimes heard·
The roar of other musketry, resounding deep and weird;
The cowboy, in the pathless wood, felt desolate and lone;
Puzzled, between two tinkling bells so very like his own!

Even the dogs, that bay the moon, were fretted into rage
By deep-mouthed blusterers, and then a canine war was waged,
Which woke the sullen hours of night, and made the welkin ring,
As if the furies, all let loose, had claimed a right to sing.

What wonder if, in ancient days, when science was unknown,
And people for mysterious things had reasons of their own,
That satyrs lived in grottoes, and wood-nymphs filled the groves,
And eldritch voices sounded from wooded dells and coves?

Translated into poetry, the German, Herder, gives
The thought, so very beautiful, which in this legend lives;
"Harmonia," Jove's agent, in framing earth and heaven,
A sound, to every living thing, had from her bosom given.

She was only half immortal, and striving thus to bless,
A sacrifice she soon became to her own tenderness;
But then, the part divine remained, and when she came to die,
She craved to visit earth unseen, and repeat her children's cry.

Jupiter touched her gently, and an echo she became,
Invisible, all-pervading, but in tenderness the same;
Where'er her children's voices sound, in sorrows, or in joys,
The mother's heart its sweetest charm of sympathy employs.

The flinty rock it pierces, and every nook and grove
Reverberant is, with cadences of pity and of love;
No discord o'er this loving harp was ever known to roll,
But every chord inclusive forms a diapason whole.

And yet she holds in strict reserve a matron's sacred claim
That Nature's law inviolate her children shall maintain;
No kind response she murmurs to those who cross her will,
Or fail to note the angles of this "Lady of the Hill"!

A shadowy lesson here we con, from old ancestral lore,
Of truth, in folly's painted guise, discussed long, long ago;
The broodings of a mother's love, symbolical, doth show
How Nature's faithful guardianship endureth evermore!

ELEGY.

LIEUT. JOHN BAYLE MORAGNE, KILLED AT THE "GARITA DE BELEN," SEPT. 13, 1847.

He hath passed away from his childhood's home,
   And from that group of love
Which clustered round the old hearthstone
   Ere any chanced to rove.
Those scattered ones may come again
   To the place they loved of yore;
But mournful will that meeting be,—
   He'll meet with them no more.

He hath passed away from the joyous throng,
   From the circles of the gay;
No eye than his more brightly shone
   In the halls of revelry.
They'll meet again, those friends he loved,
   And wear the smiles they wore;
But when they join in dance and song,
   He'll join with them no more!

He hath passed away from the martial host,
   From his place among the brave;
Their ranks are thin, their leaders lost,
   And yet their banners wave.
His own may mingle with the bands
   That rush to meet the foe;
But when they march to fife and drum
   He'll march with them no more!

ELEGY.

No more, no more, for silent now
   The voice they once obeyed;
And sadly on his pale, cold brow,
   His dark brown locks are laid.
So beautiful, so much like life,
   Yet mournful tokens tell,
That in the battle's fiercest strife
   And deadliest front he fell.

He fell! And there are some who say
   'Tis glorious thus to die,
When the gallant blood is mounting high
   In the clasp of victory;
But dearer far to me than all
   The deeds of noblest birth,
Is the gem that in his heart was worn,
   The gem of modest worth.

They tell me by the couch of pain
   He lingered long and kind,
And that his tear-drops fell like rain,
   The broken heart to bind.
They tell me that on comrade's weal
   His tenderest thoughts were bent;
And that to soothe a soldier's woe
   His little all was spent.

Oh, breathe no more that bitter boast
   Of walls and trenches gained!
So fondly loved, so early lost,
   He lies among the *slain!*
And many a comrade, brave and true,
   Lies coldly by his side.
Ah, Glory! *paledst thou not* that day
   Thy noblest victims died?

Build high, build high of marble dust,
    For the stern, unflinching great,
Whose iron steps have left no trace
    Of the heart's first tender traits;
He needs it not; within the halls
    Where his early footsteps moved
His monument is reared, and 'tis
    A *monument of love!*

GO FORWARD.

"And the Lord said unto Moses, Wherefore criest thou unto me? Speak to the children of Israel that they go forward."

"Why criest thou unto me? Have I not borne
　Thee on my bosom as a first-born son?
　In nothing have I ever said thee nay;
　And wilt thou turn thy pilgrimage to-day?
　　　　Go forward!"

"But, Lord, these craggy rocks we cannot pass,
　On each side garrisons do hold us fast;
　No ships are anchored on this ruddy sea."
"But I am here! Leave the event with me.
　　　　Go forward!"

"Ah, Lord, the hosts do tremble now with fear,
　The Egyptians' chariots are rolling near,
　The night is dark, the children weak and small."
"My name Jehova-Jireh is; fear not at all.
　　　　Go forward!"

"What! through the sea which must us all o'erwhelm?
　How shall the babes and weak the waters stem?
　These straits a snare unto thy people prove."
"I brought thee here to try thy faith and love.
　　　　Go forward!"

Pilgrims of earth, wherever you may be,
Pressed in between your "Migdols" and the sea,

Jehovah in his mercy says to you:
"Fear not; I will provide a passage through.
   Go forward!"

Man, who thy Christian journey hast begun,
And hast already many victories won,
Wouldst thou turn back this side the sea of death?
The Egyptians are behind, snares right and left.
   Go forward!

Oh, weary mother! faint and sore oppressed,
Because, as yet, thy prayers have not been blessed,
Nor fruit from tears and counsels thou canst see,
"Doubt not," thy Saviour says; "but, trusting me,
   Go forward!"

Servant of God! whose talents have been given
To rescue man from sin, and nobly striven
Without thy toil's reward, he says to thee:
"The work is thine, mine shall the issue be.
   Go forward!"

Oh! ye who walk in poverty's low vale,
The way is dark, your props and comforts fail,
And heaven seems deaf unto your helpless cry;
Look up, the Saviour speaks: "No good thing I deny.
   Go forward!"

Go forward, then, where duty's path may be.
Stand not in mute amazement by the sea
Whose floods oppose you, for your God has said:
"Up, and be doing; I the waves will tread.
   Go forward!"

Go forward to the end. His will abide
Though snares and sins beset on every side.
Press on through duty; you shall find, at last,
The waters opening for your feet to pass.
        Go forward!

THE MILLER AND THE CAMEL.

A FABLE.

There is a story told by Eastern men,
Which picturesquely describes the tempter, when,
　　With soft approaches he at first doth come
Seeking admittance to the heart, and then,
Making his most malignant purpose plain,
　　When he hath made the fortress all his own.

A miller, while his grist was running low,
Had cosily prepared to take a snore;
　　But startled from his leisure was, to see
A camel thrust his nose in at the door;
And rising quickly from the dusty floor,
　　He asked the cause of this strange mystery.

"'Tis very cold outside," the camel said,—
" I only wish to warm my nose, indeed!"
　　The miller laid him down, good easy man!
And to the camel gave no farther heed;
Who opened for himself just room to read,
　　The comfort of the refuge he would gain.

" The wind is very sharp," at length he sighed;
" Pray let me only get my *neck* inside."
　　The miller, in his dreamy mood, just now,
Could not refuse request so meekly plied,
And without more ado the door spread wide
　　Enough for crooked neck to make his bow.

The meekness of his victim suits his plan.
With modest urgency, he cries again:
  "How fast the rain-drops now begin to fall;
Though rough my coat, I am not water-proof;
Do let me place my *shoulders* 'neath your roof,—
  Grant me but this, I'll ask no more at all!"

The shoulders in, he soon forgot his vow,
And more exorbitantly growing, now,
  He asked a little, and a little more,
Till sure of his success, and seeing how
His strength would great advantages allow,
  He pushed his body quite inside the door!

No sooner thus ensconced, than growing rude,
He on the miller's comfort 'gan intrude,
  And stretched him by the fire, nothing loath.
His manners erst were very sweet and good,
But now, the miller sadly understood,
  The house was far too small to hold them both.

The rain was over, there was no excuse,
And so the miller now,— the silly goose!—
  Most civilly desired he would depart.
"Go then yourself!" replied the saucy beast.
"As for myself, I am at home, at least!
  I here shall *stay*, and act the master's part."

A camel thus knocks daily at the heart
Of all who do not choose "the better part."
  Silent and crafty does it first begin;
But growing bold, each step it gains by art
It firmly holds; nor will it thence depart
  Until entire possession it doth win!

It knocks at every door, but most, I ween,
Where are the idle and the thoughtless seen,
　Who, like the miller, taken off their guard,
Listen, half dreaming, to his specious plea,
Open the door before they *danger* see,
　And yield themselves unto a master, hard.

Then binding fast the *will*, he rules the rest
With iron sway,— no longer *guest*
　But *sovereign*, all the powers of mind obey
Implicitly his maddening, wild behest,
Till truth and virtue lose their former zest,
　And the poor soul becomes of death the prey.

THE RANCHERO'S CHILD.

From a distant ranch in the wild, wild West,—
And leaning against his stalwart breast
Was a labeled box on his saddle-bow,—
A rider came to the station's door

He was young and stout, but a haggard smile
Disfigured his face. To his gestures, wild,
His open collar, and hair unkempt,
A dark suspicion of frenzy lent.

"Is the train come in?" he asked in haste;
"For see, I have no time to waste.
This box must go, right instantly!
I will do to her as she done to me!"

"What has she done?" the agent asked,
As in the prairie sun he basked.
"You see she left me, this wife of mine,—
Went back to the East, to her folks, so fine!

"But that wasn't all!— our only child—
Deserted it, too, in the ranches wild!
The dearest, the sweetest little thing,
Just learnin' how to crow and sing!

"What could a poor young ranchman do,
Who never the ways of a baby knew?
But I bore it through heavy work all day,
And then on my bosom, at night, it lay.

"I nursed it, and fed it, but it wouldn't do,—
The little one's heart was breaking, too;—
And then, as I've heard the preacher say,—
Stranger, she was too *good* to stay!

"I've heard 'em say, and I think it's true,
God took her away. Her eyes were so blue,—
Just like her mother's,—but that wasn't much,—
Her sweet ways round my heart-strings clutch.

"I *couldn't bury her*,— I felt so bad,—
It may be, *then*, I was going mad;
For I thought I would let her mother see
I would do to her as she done to me!

"But I hear the whistle a comin' in,—
I must see her, before she *goes*, ag'in."
And the father lifted the rough deal lid
Which the pale sweet face of his baby hid,

He fell on the box with a smothered groan:
"No, stranger, I *cannot* live *alone!*
In the East my baby shall never be!
It's better for her and better for me."

So he closed the lid of the box, once more;
And in his stalwart arms he bore
The precious freight to his horse's mane,
And seizing the rein, rode home again.

Under a tree, where the sage boughs wave,
And close to his hut, he dug a grave.
A wild-rose on its bosom grew,
Weeping each morn with the evening's dew.

And on this grave, at set of sun,
When the toilsome close of the day was won,
The ranchman lay, in his lonely grief,
And talked to his darling, underneath.

SUNSET AMONG THE MOUNTAINS.

"What a pillow, embroidered of all colors, hath the dying day!"
—*Talmage.*

THE "tip-top crags" of the mountain's brow
Are gilded with transient glory now,
As the last red beams of departing day,
Striking aslant, from their turrets gray,
Through the dark green boughs of ubiquitous pine,
And where sweet stretches of vale incline,
Long lines of light and shade display!

On the tasseled floor of the forest's home,
Bright, tremulous drops of silver shone,
Playing at hide and seek, so gay!
But fled, at the night-fall's touch, away.
The starling's sweet ripple was heard just now,
Where the cool leaves weighted with moisture bow.
The flowers seem hanging their heads to weep;
And the birds have gone to their restful sleep.

But see those castles of cloud on high!
There are "burning Moscows" in the sky!
There are gardens of roses, purple and gold,
Opal and crimson; all unfold
Their softest shades, and their deepest blush,
While banners of vapor, red and flush,
Seem "warring hosts" in the evening's hush.

Oh! mineral crags, in the sunset's blaze!
Oh! cradle of clouds, in the vapory haze!
I often wonder if heaven's wall

Is more brightly burnished with gems, than all
Your castles, and turrets, and minarets bright,
Which, acting as prisms for heaven's light,
Evolve these spectrums, so fair to the sight!

I often ask if those "Mansions" fair,
Where Christ with his glorified saints appear,
Are decked in more gorgeous robes than these
That hang on the skirts of the evening breeze!
I sometimes think 'tis an angel's wing,
Opening the gates as they enter in
To meet their Lord! — those souls that shine
In the light that's borrowed from grace divine.

Or it may be the portals, left ajar
That all who so weary of darkness are
May catch a glimpse of the golden streets,
Or the jeweled throne, where amethyst meets
With jasper, and beryl, and every stone
To the bright mineralogy of heaven known,—
Where each as a chrystal mirror stands
Reflecting the face of the glorious Lamb!

MY SISTERS.

Far away in the depths of the evergreen bowers,
They lie side by side in the sweet land of flowers.
'Twas the land of their love, not the land of their birth,
And she gave them a home in her bosom of earth.

She gave them a home, but to her they had brought
No wealth, save the culture that sorrow had taught,
Of pity and kindness, refinement and truth,
And all the sweet graces of beauty and youth.

There's a song-bird that trills in the bright orange groves,
A marvel of sweetness to one that it loves;
But sweeter than all that the song-bird has trilled
Were the *voices* the Angel of Mercy has stilled.

There's a star hanging low on the blue western sky,
More steadfast and bright than all others on high,
Which sprinkle with amber and spread out a dome,
Like the wing of an angel, o'er every home.

But gentler, and sweeter, and truer, by far,
Than the song of the bird, or the light of the star,
Were the *hearts* in which home-loving virtues could blend
To form the sweet union of sister and friend!

Yet not for the welfare of kindred alone
Were their zeal and devotion so ardently shown;
They wrought for the Saviour, to whom they had given
That love which can be anchored only in heaven!

Thus heavenward bound, in the morning of life,
Our God shut them in from its cares and its strife;
And the orphans were borne to a much sweeter clime
Than any that shelves on the ocean of time.

Oh, river of lakes! on thy beautiful shore
There were visions of joy thou shalt mirror no more;
But the long moss that droops from thy shadowy trees
Sighs a requiem sad in the tropical breeze.

LINES FOR THE ALBUM OF A YOUNG FRIEND.

Come, in your life's bright morn;
Come, while the current of your life beats high;
Come, while the roses that your cheek adorn
Are radiant with the hues of hope and joy.

Bend low before his altar, meekly place
Your youth and beauty as an offering there,
And of your kind Redeemer ask the grace
To keep you from this world's bewitching snare.

Come, while your heart is free;
Come, while your thoughts are all unvexed with care;
Come, ere some earthly idol there you see
Stealing the incense which should burn in prayer.

Your best affections garner up for him
Who well deserves much more than you can give;
And, while unshackled by the cords of sin,
Resolve in your best strength for him to live.

Bring all your valued gifts;
Bring all the wealth of genius, learning, taste;
And to his service consecrating this,
A heart of pure devotion on it place.

Think not that cause demands a price too large
Which brought the King of Glory from his throne;

Nor from the *dregs of mind* that debt discharge
Which cost him *all the riches of his own.*

'Twill task the mightiest efforts of your zeal
Your own salvation to " work out " with care;
And to effect your own and neighbor's weal
The noblest energies that you can spare.

Oh! spend them not on *pleasures*, such as fill,
But never satisfy the hearts that sip,
Which, like the Dead Sea fruits, look tempting still,
But turn to worthless ashes on the lip!

But *use them for his glory*, and as gems
They'll sparkle in your coronal of youth;
And from the Master, you at length shall claim
A crown of beauty and unfading truth.

THE HUGUENOT'S FAREWELL.

Home of my youth, farewell!
  My father's home, where erst
In joy and gladness I was wont to dwell,
  And if a cloud of sadness o'er me burst
'Twas lighted by a tenderness divine,
And all of love and sympathy made mine.

The room that was mine own, the garden bowers,
  Once dear to me as the elysian fields
To the old Grecians,— others cull the flowers,
  And strangers gather up the sweets they yield.
There are no hearts within my native halls
To read the pictures graven on its walls.

The hallowed mem'ries of a hundred years!
  Breathing from stream, and dell, and forest wide,
Of those who fled from tyranny and tears,
  And found the home their God did here provide!
And these must slumber now, to wake no more
In answering tones forever; for I go,—

And with me all that hold these mem'ries dear!
  For they have faded, one by one, away,—
Those pious worshippers,— and lone and drear
  The west wind sighs above their house of clay.
Mingling with foreign tones, which seem to me
A requiem sad, home of my sires, to thee!

THE HUGUENOT'S FAREWELL.

Church of my heart, farewell,
   Church of my earliest love!
Where first devotion, in its choral swell
   Swept my young thoughts above.
What solemn whisp'rings through those sacred aisles
Bring back the guardians of my youth, whose eyes,—

If now they look on me,— I see them not
   Nor know; but ever there
A consciousness of union made the spot
   More blest than aught elsewhere.
Had we not sat together at that board,
And at that altar given our hearts to God?

But from these sacred portals I must go,
   Like some sad dove, to seek another ark,
To shelter her young nurselings from the woe
   Of friendless poverty. But hark!—
'Tis my young brothers, sleeping in their pride,
And her who bore them resting by their side.

And white-haired sire and gentle sisters call,—
   Asking reproachfully if never more
Shall tear of kindred on their marble fall;
   Nor loving fingers pluck the weeds that grow
Above their turf; No! loved ones,— No! oblivion's spell
Is deeper than the grave. Farewell! Farewell!

Land of my birth,— farewell!
   The land of heroes and of chivalry!
The many sorrows to my lot which fell
   Have not obliterated love for thee;
Yet, loving thee, I leave thee, not with pain;
For thou hast been my parent but in name!

Still, I, thy step-child, looked with honest pride
    Upon thy tree of state, so fair and high;
Whose roots, then seeking nurture, far and wide,
    Were watered with my tears in days gone by:
That blood which helped to raise its bright renown
From the best fountain of my heart was drawn.

      *   *   *   *   *   *   .

Storm-rent,— alas!— the proud Palmetto lies,
    Whose roots once wrapped thee in a cordon strong;
And jarring dissonance that harp supplies
    In other days so resonant with song;
Yet, gallant State! though prostrate in the dust
A lion's cub thou art! as at the first.

AFTER THE BATTLE.

Two young officers, seeking each other among the slain on the field of Churubusco, met unexpectedly, and fell into each other's arms and wept.

They had been friends in all their happy youth;
No bickerings foul had ever stained the truth
Of boyhood's games, or manhood's pleasant dreams;
And now, amid the harshest, bitterest scenes
Which camp life in a foreign land has shown,
That love had to a wild devotion grown,
Absorbing as the exile's dream of home,
Soft as a mother's tenderness alone;
As one when cast upon some desert strand
Hails the dear ensigns of his native land.
Saved! while the darts of death the field had swept,
What wonder if they there embraced and wept?

Around them lay the dying and the dead,
The beautiful, the brave, and they who led
The "hosts" that day,— the chieftain of the band,
And all the flower of that sunny land
Called the "Palmetto." Sorrow and despair,
Like a funereal pall, hung drooping there;
And victory its eagle pinions furled
Over the trophies of a fallen world.
Amid the dying groans, the shouts, the strife,
The anguished faces, and the joy of life,—
Saved! while so many comrades round them slept,
They rushed into each other's arms and wept!

But there were tenderer visions thronging there
Than those just born of pity and despair:
The vine-clad beauty of their sunny home,
The hills their boyish footsteps loved to roam,
The rose-wreathed porch, the parlor's dear retreat,
The clinging, fond embrace of sisters sweet,
The mother's dear, confiding, generous smile,
The father's kind, approving look, so mild,
The burning hopes of manhood, and the dreams
Which love's sweet presence wakens,—all these scenes
Tumultuous rushed before them, through the cloud
Of doubt and fear, hung o'er them like a shroud.
Saved! while these melting memories o'er them crept,
Of home and loved ones: Is it strange they *wept?*

The elder brother looked with yearning gaze,
To see the sunny glance of "other days,"
Into his brother's hazel eyes, but met
Ambition's fire. Disease had only yet
Faded the dark brown curls and paled the brow;
The warrior-spirit sparkled even now!
A span of years divided them, but then,
He to the name of brother added friend.
Oh! with a mother's thoughtful, loving care,
That brother-friend had watched him through the war!
On the last march,—'twas just the night before,—
He on his shoulders through the cañon bore
The feeble soldier, wading the cold stream
O'er the sharp pedrigral of the ravine.
The "long-roll" beat; he to his duty fled,
And left the sufferer in the cañon's bed,—
Saved! while no hope was left to them except
The hope to meet again. Oh, marvel not they wept!

Prophetic! too prophetic tears were they;
For soon upon a bed of sickness lay
The elder one. Yet, parted by the cruel chance of war
He thought not of himself, though death seemed near,
But of his brother's fate, to him unknown,
And of a mother, grieving for her son!
Thus racked he lay. One dreadful night there came
A slender, weak, attenuated frame
And sat beside the couch. Next morn
The drum's "long-roll" was beating; he was gone!
All day,—the cannon booming in his ears,—
The sick man kept grim death at bay with fears.
The firing ceased. In Montezuma's hall
Victory sat, perched upon his leaden pall;
The "hosts" within her palaces reclined;
But many a noble brave was left behind,—
Lost! while the camp fires still their vigils kept,
That night *one* brother smote his breast and wept.

THE WHITE CROSS LEAGUE.

Oh, vision of holiness, justice and truth!
Oh, beautiful compact, formed for youth;
Of virtue the very warp and woof!

Shall woman be raised to a chivalric grade,
And thou her rightful protector made
From wrongs by sore temptations swayed?

Shall a fallen brother be helped to rise,
And a hand stretched out to give the prize
To him who for this guerdon tries?

Shall vice in the scales be duly weighed,
And to either sex the same conveyed
In odium's burning fusillade?

Shall all indecorous words and songs,
And ribald jests, which to shame belong,
Be left to the coarse and vulgar throng?

Shall purity be the highest aim
Of all who hear this loyal name,
Better than honor, wealth, or fame?

Oh, league of joy! Oh, league of heaven,
If conqueror, then to thee is given
The noblest crown for which man has striven!

For of all who dwell on this weary sod,
Who sing with the gay, or in sorrow plod,
Only the pure shall rest in God!

LES BELLES AMITIÉS.

IN MEMORIAM.

MRS. M. A. WADDELL, FIRST WIFE OF DR. J. N. WADDELL, CHANCELLOR OF THE SOUTHWESTERN UNIVERSITY, TENNESSEE, FORMERLY OF SOUTH CAROLINA.

 * * *　Some pictures fair,—
Fairer than Rubens, or than Titian dreamed,—
With bright remembrances that will not sleep,
Press nightly to my pillow, in a tide
Of swelling thought which strives for utterance.

 First:
A large old church; two little fairies there,—
The one with black, the other golden hair,—
Met; and with timid glances coy and sweet,
With sweetmeats one essayed the other greet.
The pledge of amity thus eaten brought
A deathless friendship for their after years;
A spell of such exquisite pleasure wrought
A charm, so sweetly formed to lighten cares,
They, like that goddess, called the "Queen of Flowers,"
Went scattering roses through their native bowers;
Or, like a band of music down the street,
Flinging out sweetness unto all who meet.

Again: The Academia's pleasant shades,
Where, through the whole long summer eve,
The slanting sunbeams waited for the hour

Of "recess" for these two, when, hand in hand,—
The curt'sy at the door being duly paid,—
They sought, with loving housewif'ry, the stores
Of shells and china 'neath the mossy trees.

Then, sweet girlhood's rosy hours —
The garden walk by moonlight; or the 'stroll
Along the river's brink; the ramblings in the woodland
While the dew still gemmed the flowers; oftenest
On some old gnarled root or swinging bough,
Reading aloud the " tales of other days."
'Twas beautiful to see them, hand in hand,
Culling each beauty from fair Nature's dower;
'Twas beautiful to see their minds expand,
Extracting wisdom from each classic flower;
Sipping, like butterflies, the stores that lie
In the enchanted realms of Poesy;
Gathering, like bees, the " Hybla" sweets that dwell
In the old sage's geometric cells.
* * *   Each leaning on the other, day by day,
They mounted to the skylights which unrolled
Such drifts of glory on their youthful souls,
That, while God's sunlight sweetly on them shone,
They gave to others' hearts what blessed their own.

* * *   The scene was changed:
She from her maiden joy was early won,
Life's glad, but graver, duties to fulfill.
A bridal wreath was thrown
Over the childish brow of sweet sixteen.
    And so she went,
To make her bower beneath a Western star.
She went, like Abra'am, nothing in her hand
But trust; and leaning upon this,

She turned her back forever on the hearth
Which once had warmed her: and the playmate dear
Of happy childhood days — her hand in his,
Not knowing what might yet befall her there.
And this is woman's faith! But oft, I ween,
Memory played truant to the busy scenes
Of household love, and visited the shades
On her own hillside, 'neath the waving trees,
Where, book in hand, they dreamed away the hours,
Or caught the echoes in the sounding hall
Made vocal with the youthful laugh and song.

* * * They met once more on earth, and only once.
More spiritual in its soft matron beauty
It had grown, that young wife's face!
The noble brow looked holier, sadlier;
The once laughing eyes
Seemed gazing, seer-like, into worlds unknown!
That golden key which unlocks all the wards
Of the heart's cells had opened to her gaze
The heritage of sorrow we have won
From sin and death. One fair boy,
Who, a few summers, nestled near her heart,
The Shepherd of the flock had bid her lay
In his own bosom. This duty done,
She meekly kissed the rod, and followed on,
With soft and quiet tread, the toddling steps
Of a sweet cherub girl.
With meek acceptance she endured, or took
All that the Shepherd gave, and followed still
Through gifts or through denials.
And now, with loving zeal, she strove to lead
The "sister of her soul" unto that fount
Whence she had drawn such draughts of patient love,

Obedience, and faith.
Her gentle pleadings she essayed in words
Like Moses' to his friend: "'Come, go with me;
The Lord hath spoken good concerning those
Who seek his love.' One we have ever been
In hopes and joys,— shall we be parted now?"

* * * Again farewell was said: she to her home
Returned, and to its quiet duties, all fulfilled
As standing in the presence of her God.
But, though in patience she so far excelled,
Abating not one jot of all that fell
Unto her lot, she seemed not all of earth.
        One ear was turned
To hear the bleating of her lamb above;
And so, after a few short years of duteous toil,
The Shepherd kindly took *her* to his fold.
Thus early went she from her trial proof,
Leaving behind this witness upon earth.
        In purity and truth,
In zeal for souls, she stood alone!
Beauty may win, and genius more may charm;
    "Take her for all and all,
We ne'er shall look upon her like again!"

* * * Now as the shadows lengthen 'neath the feet
Of the survivor, memory fonder grows,
And more intense and irrepressible the wish to look,
As once she looked, upon that angel face.
        The birds recall her,
And the low, rich sound of tinkling rivulets;
The stars from heaven seem to speak of her;
And dearer and more urgent grows the thought
That they *must* meet again,

Who loved on earth so purely.
The vine, grown over on the garden wall,
Though rooted here,
Will bud and blossom on the other side!

UNFORGOTTEN THINGS.

As TRAVELERS over burning sands
   Pine for the purling streams,
So they, who on life's margin stand,
   Yearn for their early dreams.
Sweet voices, but not heard for years,
   Come through the shadowy gloom
Of wasted hopes and bitter tears,
   And whisper, softly, "Home."
Then, seated at our mother's knee,
   The world looks bright again;
And eyes speak only truthfully;
   And hearts are free from pain.

They come, the fair, the brave, the good,
   Who trod our paths of old;
We hear the laugh of maidenhood —
   That music of the soul!
The singing birds, the tinkling brooks,
   Glad thoughts again can weave;
We lie within the mossy nooks
   Beneath the rustling leaves;
The wild flowers, with their tangles bright,
   Breathe fragrance round us yet;
And on the starry brow of Night
   Beauty and Love are met.

Nor do we now forget the joy
   When Knowledge first unrolled
Her ample page; when Science coy
   Poured out her pearls and gold;

When Music woke an infant lyre
   Within our heart of hearts;
And Beauty brought poetic fire
   To touch the strings of Art.
Oh, blessed lore of things Divine,
   Which Nature's arms enfold!
Bright jewels from the eternal mine,
   Laid in the ages old!

But garnered up with tenderest care
   Among my precious things,
Are faces which for me would wear
   The smile approval brings;
The trust in what I seemed,— the love
   That could opine no blame
In faults which might all others move
   To pity or condemn.
There's not a tone or thought which claimed
   An interest in my lot,
There's not a wish, by Friendship framed,
   My heart remembers not!

The glowing tints of "Love's young dream"
   My memory must retain;
Like sunset waves its beauty seems
   On Evening's dark domain.
That sun of life is going down;
   But ever, on my soul,
The thrill it woke in days by-gone,
   In tidal wave doth roll.
The long, long years of faithfulness,
   Which never brought regret,
The voice that only spoke to bless,—
   How could I e'er forget?

The mariner far out at sea
    Heeds not the landsman's mirth;
His eyes are fixed adoringly,
    But not on things of earth.
Thus, through the mists and storms of time,
    My Pole-star shines above,
Kindling a glow of thought sublime,
    A sense of pardoning love!
Cold be my heart as nether stone,
    From thought and memory free,
If ever I forget to own
    What Jesus did for me!

THE GLORY AND THE GRIEF.

I saw it in my dreams,— a face
   I had not seen for years;—
   'Twas beautiful, though seen through tears;
For thoughts, long buried, came apace,—

In rainbow visions, hued with gold;—
   As clouds that scud before the wind
   Fly swiftly, and no more are seen,
Leaving the sky so gray and cold,—

Thus quickly fled my new delight—
   And left a blank within my soul;
   For all at once he seemed so old!
His manner void of softness — quite.

He clasped my hand in jejune haste.
   What was there ominous in this
   To treasures of remembered bliss
When he was young and full of grace?

When in the rosy hours of youth
   We drank in beauty with the flowers
   And thought all hearts as pure as ours
And all the world as full of truth!

"Is earth alone the scene of love?
   Do all emotions of the heart
   From off the spirit's glow depart
When transferred to the worlds above?"

'Twas mildly asked,— and as I gazed,
　His features hard and stony grew;
　"No matter, I am aged, too!
And now in winter's purple haze."

We stood apart. But as I conned
　The wonder o'er, it seemed to me
　The picture showed what he should be
If to this world he had belonged.

And now, again, the mirror smiled
　As o'er it swept a vision fair:
　He in his youth was pictured there!
And I to death was reconciled.

Immortal beauty I could trace,—
　Immortal virtue in his eye,
　And tenderness that could not die
Daguerrotyped upon his face.

And I to death was reconciled;—
　For then I saw, that Love Divine,
　Which so much tenderer was than mine
Had from the woes of earth beguiled—

His soul away to distant skies,
　Where beauty never could grow less,
　Nor age make hard, nor want distress,
Nor life become a thing despised.

LINES TO A MAGNOLIA BUD.

SENT FROM SOUTH ALABAMA BY MY LITTLE FRIENDS, GEORGE AND FRANK M——.

Sweet flow'ret of our Southern soil,
   Opening thy petals fair,
Above our Country's sin and toil,
   Like Hope, above despair.

Blest token of our Father's love;
   Who, when this world of ours
So recreant to its trust had proved,
   Still left with us the flowers.

Thou bringest back the joy of old
   When I was young and gay;
Some things have faded from my soul,
   But this can ne'er decay.

Yet, brighter than thy snowy plumes,
   And richer than thy leaves,
More fragrant than the sweet perfume
   Thou waftest on the breeze,—

The kindly thought that sent thee here,
   My sorrows to assuage,—
That reverence is, of all, most dear,
   Which childhood gives to age.

And thus, my little friends, may all
   Your actions blessings be,

And all your future life recall
   What you have done for me!

Love God, love Nature, and love Truth,
   Love all that God has made;
And with the innocence of youth
   Let manhood be arrayed.

So, like the grand magnolia tree,
   Where grace and beauty blend;
In every aspect you may be
   The type of Southern men!

THE BABY.

INSCRIBED TO "CLARA LOUISE," MY FIRST
GRANDCHILD.

Thou precious one, that liest on my knee
Passive and sweet! Oh, what is life to thee,
    So seemingly incognizant of all
Around thee here? Thou charming mystery,
Do any inklings of the things that be
    Upon thee fall?

Sweet germ of being! keenly dost thou hear,
And yet my words fall senseless on thy ear,
    A mere refrain
That gives no thought to thee, my baby dear,
Of love, or hope, or anxious mother-care,
    Of joy or pain.

Thou comprehendest not? Then why that smile
Flitting so strangely bright, my cherub child,
    Across thy face?
Do seraph voices, whispering all the while,
Attend, thy vacant hours to beguile
    With angel grace?

Or do the harmonies from whence thou came
Breathe on thy new-born ear the sweet acclaim
    Of Eden's bowers?
Ah, dear one! many discords thou wilt gain
By venturing upon this world of pain,
    This world of ours!

Linked, as thou art, half way between the two,
By smiles and tears, thou hast both worlds in view.
      A little space,
'Twill not be long, for things both strange and new
Will soon the image of the fair and true
      From thee efface.

E'en now thou openest wide thy lustrous eyes,
At every sight and sound, in sweet surprise,
      Seeming to look away
Into the unknown past; but thou art growing wise
In pantomime, and soon will wear the guise
      Of one whom present things will oft bewray.

Ah me, the rush of new sensations is too much!
Thou *sighest*, my darling! 'Tis the first light touch
      Of Sorrow's trills;
Oh, born to trouble, feelest thou, then, so soon,
The jar of earth? And bearest thou the doom,
      So early, of its ills?

Well, rest thee now, sweet baby, in these arms,
In blest unconsciousness of life's alarms,
      And gather strength
To take in, one by one, the fleeting charms,
And meet with stronger nerve the many harms
      Which come at length.

Rest, little stranger! Though there's much of woe,
And many thorns will in thy pathway grow,
      Even from thy birth;
Yet, life hath choicest blessings to bestow,
And thou, if pure and true, much joy may know
      While on this earth.

THE BOTANIC RAMBLE.

A REMINISCENCE.

I.

A SOUTHERLY breeze, and a cloudless sky;—
And we sallied forth, the children and I;
The air was so soft, and the sky was so blue,
The young hearts so rapt with emotions new,
For 'twas in the beautiful month of June,
And the woods were fragrant with rich perfume.

II.

Tackle for fishing, and baskets, too!
More than *one* purpose we had in view.
From school-room studies some maidens came,
Seeking, in Flora's wide domain,
Subjects for thought. As I sat by the brook,
Watching a minnow that nibbled my hook,
Little Pierre, at the end of his line,
Flourished a mud cat. "It is mine!" "It is mine!"
The children shouted; and then, amain,
A deep hollow murmur in syllables came,
"Mine — mine." In fearful dread
The little ones gathered around. I said,
In questioning accents: "Who are you?"
The answer came mockingly back: "You — you."
Again I questioned: "And shall we come?"
Clear was the soft response: "Come! — come!"
So we went through the trackless woods unknown
To knock at the door of the wood-nymph's home.

III.

Our little fat terrier ran on before
Shaking his silky black curls all o'er;
And the deep wood uttered a musical roar,
As if a half dozen dogs or more
Were storming a fortress in the dell;
But when for us the drawbridge fell,
The children were much surprised to find
That no answer came to their summons kind;
For though so garrulous when alone—
To callers, the "Lady" is "*not at home.*"
Nevertheless, beside the door
Was a "Golden Slipper"* as bright, I'm sure,
As the fairy shoe which the young "Prince" put
On poor little "Cinderella's" foot.

IV.

Climbing the flowery turrets up,
The "Lady" we robbed of her "Painted Cup,"†
And the ferns which compose her braided hair,
And the "Bridal Wreath"‡ she was wont to wear.
Young "Aspidiums," exquisitely curled,
Were peeping out; but the social world
Of "Convallarias," "Poligalas" too,
"Uvularias" bright, and "Violas" blue,
Had passed their early pupilage,
And now were storing up fruits for age.

V.

On the rustic bridge we were bidding farewell,
But the "Dryads" held us in mystic spell.
How happy we were! The hills were blue

---

* Cypepedium pubescens.
† Euchromia pallens.
‡ Tiarella cordifolia.

With that hazy, soft, enchanting hue
Midsummer gives. The tremulous air,
The soothing hum of the locust's bore,
Blent with the smaller, sweeter notes
Of insects filling their tuneful throats
From honey-cupped flowers. Ever and anon
The starling shook his exquisite trombone,
The red-bird trilled his varied lay,
The woodpecker whetted his scythe so gay!
The watchman's whistle the king-bird blew,
And the mocking-bird rendered them all anew.

VI.

Sauntering on, in this happy mood,
We entered a long, low, level wood,
Where the trees stood up, distinct and tall,
Shedding sweet glimpses of sky on all
The islets and geometric forms
Which the meandering stream had worn.
Mosaiced in patterns from Nature learned,
Were " Hepaticæ," mosses, and feathery ferns.
Tall pines, whose roots were washed by the stream,
Wore a carpet of wreaths of the "Ivy" green.
Mitchella's lowly twin velvety flower
And its scarlet berries, in their leafy bower,
Clustered like gems. Our "Fernery," dear,
We 'plenished with delicate traceries here;
Content, in our homeward path, to scan
How nature a transcript is of man.

VII.

"Viburnums" had dropt their petals fair,
As faded and useless for future wear,
And now, in earnest, had set about
Bringing their horde of capsules out.

"Andromeda's" leathery bells were few;
But round an "Æsculus glabra" flew
A thousand tiny, gauzy things.
And humming-birds, with their rainbow wings,
Twirling and singing in insane glee,—
Like many Bacchanals we see,—
Inserting their bills in the nectared horns
Of the splendid flower which this tree adorns.

VIII.

Over the hill, as we drew near home,
The setting sun in its glory shone.
Seemingly borne on its last red beam
Came a strain as sweet as a Moslem's dream;
'Twas a chorus of youthful voices, nigh,
Enjoying their work 'neath the open sky.
The jubilant notes of "Bonny Eloise"
Came trippingly back on the evening breeze.
Entranced we stood, in doubt to ken
Which was the sweeter, the song, or then,
Good "Mother Harmonia," deliciously coy,
Repeating the sound of her children's joy!

THE VILLAGE CHURCH BELL.

WRITTEN UNDER DEEP AFFLICTION.

SLOWLY and dreamily it comes,
  Through the dim openings of the forest aisles;
Now hushed, now swelling up in freshened tones,
  Peal upon peal resounding through the wilds,
Still ringing soft and clear above the sound
Of sad winds, sobbing in the dark pines round.

So musically sweet! — yet, to my heart
  It seems, — in concert with the wood's low sigh, —
To breathe that sorrow which his mortal part
  Wrung from the "Friend of Sinners" in the cry, —
Alas! how thrills mine own in sympathy, —
"My God! my God! hast thou forsaken me?"

The only link that bound me to the past,
  The only sound which spoke to me of heaven.
And now 'tis gone! I knew it could not last,
  That dream of earthly sweetness which had risen
Time's touch is real. Here, without relief,
Benumbed I sit, — *alone*, with my *great grief!*

How deep the gloom! This leaden silence falls
  Incubus-like, upon my heavier soul,
Curdling the quivering pulse, which over all
  The strings of joy once swept without control.
The harp that once held rapture in its flow
Lies *crushed*, 'neath *Fate's inexorable blow.*

Yet, blessed chime! thy prophet tones inspire
    Thoughts of that "better land" where grief is hushed,
And of that tree which heals with sweet'ning power
    The bitter streams which from our hearts have gushed.
Then trill those symphonies;—though not for me,
For *others* wake your Gospel minstrelsy!

Tell of a Saviour's love, and let the tale,
    So true and wonderful, arrest the feet
Of many, wandering far from Wisdom's pale,
    Who here shall come, their "Sacrifice" to greet.
Thus to the woes of earth shall peace be given,
And all our *weary* thoughts find *rest in heaven*.

EDGEFIELD, SOUTH CAROLINA, 1862.

CONSIDER THE LILIES.

A PARAPHRASE.—Matt. vi. 28-30.

"Consider the lilies," the Saviour said,
    As on the mount, near Genesaret,
He looked on the autumn fields, o'erspread
    With bright "Amaryllis luted," yet,—

"Consider" them, not as a whole; take one,
    Examine its petals; softer far
Than the softest velvet by artists spun,
    And richer than drops of amber are!

The splendid versatile authors see
    On their slender filaments, ready to burst
And scatter their treasure wide and free
    In golden farinaceous dust,—

See the triple-crowned style, which, in its turn,
    Conveys the life-giving pollen down
To the nascent seed in the three-valved germ
    In the lowest sheath of the calyx found.

"Consider the lilies!" Look closer yet:
    A secluded nectariferous gland
In the base of each bright claw is set,
    Filled with perfume from your Father's hand!

The lilies! They neither toil nor spin,
    Yet are they clothed in raiment free;

And fairer than all that gold could win
   For Solomon's glorious majesty!

If the grass of the field, which dies so soon,
   If a spire of moss that is scarcely seen
And lies in the highway's dust at noon,
   Wear a Divine impress within,—

Much more for you, oh, faithless one!
   Whose mission of soul must last for aye,
For whom the Father gave his Son,
   Shall he his wisdom and care display.

This beautiful sermon on trust, we find,
   Is just as potent for you and me,
And for all who to doubt his love incline,
   As when spoken first in sweet Galilee!

How happy, if, when our faith is lost,
   We could trace his love in each flower we see,
And say: "He feedeth the tiny moss,
   And surely, he will remember me!"

JACOB AT THE WELL.

SOME things there are in heaven's wondrous plan
Which fill us with sublime delight,— and then
With silent awe, when Sovereign Love unfolds
His tender purposes for sinful man.

When Jacob, leaning on his pilgrim's staff,
Beside the ancient well in Haran stood,—
    Pondering his deep regret,—
The same, and yet, another man he was!
That Love Divine which had rebuked his course,
Had, in its wise omniscience, given him peace.
        But then, alas!
The serpents which had so beset his path,—
They stung him sorely yet!
Wrapt in a sombre spell,—
Musing,— he saw again his mother's tent,
And all the years of luxury and ease
Which forfeit were by his own selfish act.
In panoramic view, most sadly sweet,
Rose Canaan's lovely vales and sunny hills;
But like an ogre there,
Eating into his heart, was Esau's famished mien,
And the vile trade,— so unfraternal!
With the pottage red. Unbidden came
His artful schemings, and his mother's guile,
Seeking by treachery to invest with power
Her favorite child: The parleyings,—
The dark deceit,— the flight,—
The old blind father's tears were wearing still
Upon his heart, as water wears the stone.

The dismal lodging in a place so drear,
Shunning the paths to the pursuer known,
Behind him lowered dark a life-long dread,
While doubt and danger loomed up far ahead.
Then came the ladder, touching earth and heaven,
And angels going up and coming down,
Silently ministering of heaven's lore
To this poor stricken one!
   The wonder grew
Into a span of hope, so beautiful!
It stirred the bosom of the exiled man,
Flying from just revenge, and under ban
Of home and friends,— such pitying love to see,—
A mystery, born in the ages old,
That God, in his electing love, should choose
One who in his inherent right no merit had,
One who to truth had given so little heed,
And who the evil arts of Nature used
To sate his earthly greed!
It stirred his bosom with a sense of wrong,
  And ill desert,—
To that contrition which a rebel feels
When conscious guilt to sovereign mercy yields,
And leaves the obdurate heart attuned to praise.
   Now he could say with joy:
"Surely, none other than the house of God this is
And this the gate of heaven!"

Never before to Jacob's worldly sense
Had this bright gate appeared;
Although to win his wayward sons to heaven
The poor old Patriarch tried;
And with this light there came a clearer view
Of all the Abra'amic covenant implied,
Learned at his grandsire's knee,

But feebly understood and carnally
Construed to suit his avarice and pride.
              Now too late
He saw his weakness and its forfeiture:
An outcast from his home and heritage,
And doomed a bitter conflict to endure,
Long years of toil and weary vassalage!
            Humbled, but wiser now,
His heart was ready to record that vow
In covenant with his great Almighty Friend,
Who, when by all he had forsaken been,
Had "taken him up" with promises Divine.
            Then as he journeyed on
His step grew lighter, as his faith grew strong;
But earthlier feelings, with the ties of home,
Still to his spirit clung. He thought of all
His mother's doting love,—
    So self-forgetting,—
And his heart was wrung
With anguish for that poor mistaken one,
Now 'reft of both her sons, the sequence sad
Of weak indulgence in parental love!

BESIDE THE SYRIAN WELL.

FOOT-SORE and thirsty, as he took his stand,
A stranger in his mother's native land!
That utter helplessness the cynic feels,
    Alone in crowds,
Came o'er his soul; but with a sudden bound
His pulses leap exultingly!
When to his questioning the shepherds tell:
"Yes, this is Laban's well,
And lo! his daughter cometh with the sheep!"
        O'er Jacob's heart
Its sweet illusions Love had never thrown.
Ishmael's young daughters and the maids of Heth
Might try in vain the Hebrew prince to snare;
Rebecca's counsels, and the pride of self
Had kept him heart-whole though the maids were fair.
        Now love and duty proved
All the long pent-up wishes in his breast
Could in delicious rapture be exprest!

With virgin mood, and brightly braided hair,
With sweet simplicity and winning grace,
And conscious beauty shining in her face,
This youthful shepherdess a conqueror came!
    To Jacob's 'wildered brain,
O'erwhelmed with wonder and delight and shame.
She mirrored all the visions he had kept
Of love and home; and so the marvel came
That this coincidence of time and place
Awakened all the feelings which had slept
      Incipiently,—

And as the beauteous damsel he embraced,—
While these conflicting thoughts his bosom swept,—
He lifted up his manly voice and wept!
       Some one has said:
"He who would wish a fond full heart to gain
Must seek it when 'tis sore, allay its pain
With love by pity prest,—'tis all his own."
          This, Rachel's pity and her beauty did
For the poor stricken fugitive, and wove
A witching sorcery, so *deeply* wove
That twice seven years of savage toil but proved
A scanty measure for his boundless love.

TALLULAH.

I.

THE traveler, as he wends his eager way
   Toward Nature's temple, great Niagara,
Hears from afar its thundering echoes play —
   Hoarse-sounding, in their elemental war.
And thus his soul is girded up to weigh
The power, which, unforeseen, would on his spirits prey,
   Bearing them down with an excess of awe;
But nerves him, bye and bye, for the sublime
"Te Deum" on this grand old harp of time!

II.

Not so where Southern breezes blow,— amid
   The Unacaya Mountains; there,
Within a gorgeous forest, deeply hid,
   Where no monitions of the stream appear,
Terrora* winds in silent beauty, rid
Of all earth's garish sounds. And never did
   A scene more strangely fair
Burst on the view,— not e'en from Alpine height
Or the deep gorges which the eye delight,—

III.

Or shock with grandeur, on the lofty range
   Of Himalayan glaciers, cleft apart
By Nature's hammer-men. With feelings strange,
   We view this work of superhuman art,

---

* "Terrora," the Indian name for "terrible."

Glossed by six thousand years, without a change
Its adamantine pillars to derange.
How does the thought appall the human heart!
Standing upon a little span of earth,
We look aghast, and wonder at thy birth.

IV.

Terrible stream! Not terrible art thou,
  Save in the breadth and depth which hems thee in
Thy rocky palaces, where spruce-firs bow
  Their graceful branches, softly penciling
Green shadows on the purple rocks and o'er
The golden mosses, with their crimson spores,
  A canopy of fadeless beauty throw.
Down, down, a thousand feet, thou seem'st asleep,
Voiceless Terrora, in thy home so deep!

V.

Silent and shadowy, as the forms that flit
  Over the juggler's mirror, thou dost seem
Voluptuousness enshrined, or, better yet,
  The sweet illusion of a poet's dream.
Beneath our feet a fairy isle, a "Liliputian" forest gem is set
Within thy bright reflections. There are met
  The arching bough and silvery leaf of green,
While pensile wreaths and mossy rings in flocks
Climb up, and tapestry the craggy rocks.

VI.

Nature reposes; but like the "Glen-Almain," where
    Ossian sleeps,
  "It is not quiet — is not ease,"
That reaches up from the far sleepy depths, and keeps
  In the vast solitude its charmed levees,

With wonder, and that sense which only weeps
When filled to overflowing from the deeps
　　Of mystery and beauty. Tokens, these,
That Nature brings to our remorseful eyes,—
The dower of sadness gained in paradise.

VII.

Away, where yonder rocky turrets rise,—
　　The long-continuous chasm opening free,—
Looming up grandly 'gainst the distant skies
　　Losing themselves in great immensity!
We long to follow on, as flies
The eagle to the sun; but vainly tries
　　Our earthly thought to grasp eternity!
Like that same eagle struggling in his moil,
We flap a broken wing within our mortal coil!

VIII.

"To sit on rocks, to muse o'er flood and fell,"
　　In solitude, is all the cynics boast;
But surely, if the friends we love so well
　　Are dear at any time, we love them most
When silence spreads o'er river, rock, and dell,
Soft draperies, with not a sound to tell
　　Of human sympathies, and all the host
Of weird emotions, pent up in the soul —
Pain, with excess of pleasure, uncontrolled.

IX.

Mysterious silence! Who shall dare to look
　　Into thy sacred oracle? As yet
Thou hast within thy hand a sealed book,
　　Coeval with eternity. The chiming cascade whets
Its own eulogium. The babbling brook
Tells its own tale. The sea, in every nook,

Murmurs in self-applause, or moaning frets.
Thou Goddess! with thy finger on thy lip,
Canst make the blood within our vitals creep!

X.

Give me, then, to share this weight of beauty, such
    a band
  Of friends; not thoughtless, gay, nor frivolously
    dull;
Not stupidly phlegmatic; not the bland
  But earnest worshipper of Nature, full
Of mild enthusiasm, formed to scan
The slightest shades of coloring,— the minute man,
  Contemplative, to whom there's nothing null
In all God's works; who sees the hand
Of Wisdom tracing out the wondrous plan.

XI.

With such I'd love to wander on for days,
  Up the terrific cliff-side, seeking out,
As in a book of prints, each glowing page,
  Or drinking "Linked sweetness long drawn out."
With such I once essayed the shelving edge
Of the rude precipice, and stumbling down the ledge,
  Seated us, sadly wearied, on a rock,
The blue sky looking down, our eyes to greet,
The fair Tallulah tossing at our feet.

XII.

Hemmed in those granite walls, 'twas sweet to prove
  A perfect isolation from the ills
That make us sorrow in the world above.
  But by the boulders stopped against our wills—
How longed I for a magic barque, to move

Beneath the shadows of the emerald grove,
   Under a charmed spell of safety, still,
And ever gliding on the beauteous stream,
Drink to my fill of Pleasure's 'witching dream!

XIII.

With such a band of friends I fain would stand
   Upon the rocky " pulpit " jutting o'er
The yawning gulf. A chasm on each hand,
   Inspiring terror seldom felt before.
But never yet did poet's dream expand
In Tuscan valleys, or sweet " Tempe's " land,
   A scene more lovely than the vale below;
Here, 'neath the fairy trees, three cascades peep,
Foaming and sparkling and yet fast asleep,—

XIV.

As in a magic mirror; for no sound
   Comes floating on the balmy air, so high,
Nor breaks the illusion of the depths profound,
   Which all in panoramic beauty lie.
Enchanting softness settles all around,
And a blue hazy veil is richly thrown
   Over the creeping plants and rocks of amber dye,
While right and left the ragged ramparts rise,
Painting their gorgeous tints against the azure skies.

XV.

A little farther on,— we reach the place
   Where the crags bolder rise, and less inclined;
And near the top an aperture we trace,
   In which the eagle made her nest " Lang Syne."
Here, one, who proved most daring of his race,
Ventured the frightful quarry's mouth to face,

All slippery with the tassels of the pine.
He who at last, to ruin Fame's fleeting breath,
In the "Alamo" met a cruel death.

XVI.

Over the mountain ledge, press on, and lo!
  The rich low bass tones of an organ hymn,
Welling up sweetly from the vale below,
  Through the high trees the waters glistening.
Descend we now, a hundred feet or more,
Where the green waters from their chalice pour
  In one delicious bound against the rim
Of the huge rock, and fall,— a graceful shower
Of diamond drops, into their muffled bower!

XVII.

Guarded within this fastness from the world,
  Unique in beauty, simple, pure, and grand,
Convulsion's fragments all around thee hurled,
  How dost thou mock the arrogance of man?
Pride cannot solve the problem here so old;
Ambition cannot grasp a gulf so bold,
  Nor Canute-like its majesty command.
And man, whate'er he is in "court, camp, grove,"
The pigmy of creation here must move.

ALGÆ.

A FRAGMENT.

Is THERE no algæ, except in the sea?
Yes, dear, in all quiet waters there be
Germs floating, invisible, through the air,
Awaiting moisture and rest.   Like hair,
Or sprouting in feathery flakes, they cling
To rocks that are washed by a brook or a spring.
A stone that is placed in an eddying stream
Becomes slippery with this algæ green.
On the damp garden path where the sun seldom shines,
On the walls of a house that is mouldy with time,
Is a delicate sod, formed of myriad germs,—
Incipient plants,— with a texture firm.
All nature these infinite spores pervade.
They are found in old fissures in cheeses made,
Rising from corks in the wine-cellar's stand;
In graceful festoons from the ceiling they hang;
The mouldiness seen on a worthless old shoe
Is a forest of algæ, curious to view!
Sucked up in water-spouts, carried by winds,
The unique phenomenon, red snow, we find
In a cloud of these spores from the Arctic fields,
Which this species of "musci" so lavishly yields.
On mountain crags, or on the stones of the brook,
There is often a tracery of purplish look;
Or rose-colored filaments floating, we see,
In the beautiful order, "convervoidæ."

Of what use, then, are these germs to man?
Ask of what use is the fruitful rain,

Which fills the dried-up streams, in time
To soften with mists an arid clime.
As mist to the parched atmosphere,
This algæ is to all being here.
Its mission all *Nature's waste* restores;
Beauty in barrenness from it flows;
Fertility from desolation springs,
As *life* to the sterile rock it brings!
Wherever there's dampness, on roof or rock,
These tiny green films are seen to flock.
The little rootlets dig deeply down,
Where moisture, held by their fronds, is found.
When the stems decay, the débris forms soil;
And the softened rock, in its constant toil,
Triturates into a fertile field;
And the barren stones, and the rough earth yield
"To starred divisions of rubied bloom,
To fringes of amber and silver,"— soon
To a mantle of beauty and grace, so bright
That the greenness of earth is a long delight!

But this is not all. At the roots of trees,
In the glens, among ferns, and things like these,
The sheaths and calyptras collect the rain,
And *feed it out* to the earth again.
When more they cannot hold, the drops
Trickle in rivulets, forming brooks;
And thus, by the moss-beds in mountains spread,
Our glorious rivers and lakes are fed.
"How beautiful!" you are apt to say,
"The part which those tiny mosses play!"
But there's a more touching, tenderer view;
For the mosses put on their greenest hue
When the trees are drest in their livery gray,
And summer and flowers have passed away.

Unlike the heartless summer friend,
They to adversity courage lend,
And over the wrecks and ruins of time,
A green loving wreath of charity twine.
The woods and the blossoms have done their part;
But the "slow-fingered" mosses, with constant heart,
Over the head-stones, watch and wave
"Flowers for the bride's chamber,—*moss for the grave.*"

SCENE ON THE HUDSON.

ENGRAVING IN AN ALBUM.

BEAUTIFUL Hudson! Many speak of thee,
As boldly on thou rushest to the sea
From out thy mountain home, where proudly rise
Thy purple rocks and rose bays to the skies.
Let *others praise* thee; for the sunset gleam,
Settling upon thy waters, wakes a dream
From the deep shade of that embattled hill,
So sad and mournful that my heart is still
And mute of eulogy. It speaks of one,
Who, in the radiance of his life's bright morn,
Looked on thee with exulting pride, though far
His home was sheltered 'neath a Southern star;
And found amid thy beauties joys as true
As ever youth and generous manhood knew.

How like it seems, as in those days when he
Heard the sweet music of the "Reveille,"
Or bending o'er thy waters caught the sound
Where boatman's whistle broke the echoes round.
The little sails he loved so well are there,
Filled with the spiced breath of the mountain air,
And lie reflected on the glassy tide,
Or else exulting o'er the waters ride.
There are the friends his heart was formed to prize,—
Sketching, as he would sketch, the rocks and skies.
But when I ask for him whose bounding heart
Bore in these pleasures such a rapturous part,
The mountains answer in their robes of green:

"An end of all perfection we have seen!"
Sweet Hudson! though responsive to thy praise,
I may not speak as erst in happier days;
And though, alas! with patriot pride, no more
Can I look on thee, as I've looked before;
Yet, richly art thou fraught with thoughts of him
Who called me "sister," and though faint and dim
The mem'ries thou dost bring; still, as they come
Mingling with all the sorrows I have known
Through the long lapse of years,— the best relief
This scene affords me, is *the joy of grief!*

WASHINGTON IRVING.

Thou master of a spirit-stirring spell,
  Waking the thoughts to either grief or glee,
Whether of joy or woe thy numbers tell;
  They breathe a strain of noblest minstrelsy!

'Tis thine to prove the sovereignty of mind,
  Based on the purity of feelings high,
To show how man may mingle with his kind,
  And only be a profiter thereby.

Thy morning dreams were speedily fulfilled;
  Thou didst stand wondering on a foreign shore,
But foreign lands, nor foreign arts, were skilled
  To spoil a mind so pure and bright before.

It is a glorious privilege to be
  Endowed with feelings and a gift like thine,
Whose bright reflections turn to poetry
  All thoughts and things, whichever way they shine.

Old England's rural haunts and honest hearts,
  Grenada's rosy founts and marble halls,
The Dutchman's legends, and the Spaniard's arts,
  Are bathed in light which from thy genius falls.

Who would not be a traveler with thee,
  Wrapt in so soft a visionary shroud
Of beauty, like some golden hues, we see,
  Shrined in the halo of a sunset cloud?

Of good and beautiful the world owes much
  To thy exalted mind and perfect taste;
And yet it knows not which has mostly touched,
  Thy gentle goodness, or poetic grace.

Surely life is blest to thee! thus sweetly bound
  In bright imagination's golden zone.
It *must* be joy, to know that naught is found
  In all thy works which *thou wouldst blush to own*.

OUT OF THE DEPTHS.

On hearing a sermon from the words: "The heart knoweth its own bitterness."

OH, PITYING One! my wearied heart sinks down
   In voiceless agony beneath thy feet.
In all the world no solace can be found
   To make my inward anguish incomplete.

In vain my tongue would try, in melting tones,
   To touch a chord in unison with woe;
All echoless, and sepulchred in groans,
   The secret is unfathomed as before.

Tears coursing down my cheek may witness seem
   Of grief too deep for words; but overflow,
As well it may, no unscathed heart can know
   How deep and dark the gulf still lies below.

The sighs that heave and rend my tortured breast,
   Won from the smould'ring fires pent within,
But futile breathings are of that sad quest
   Made for deliverance from grief and sin.

Nature may fail, the over-burdened heart
   Falter and stop beneath the heavy strain;
But life flows back, intent to do its part
   In keeping up the *ministry of pain*.

My grief! My grief! The world, in busy greed,
   Careless and selfish, rushes madly by;

No time *it* has to give the way-worn heed,
　And only to the *gladsome* makes reply.

My bosom friend,—one I had fondly tried,
　Essays with smiles to charm away my care;
No love, nor counterfeits, can set aside
　The trouble which *another may not share*.

Oh, guilt may hide, and pride may stifle in
　The sorrows that would only meet disdain.
The sorest grief of all that's born of sin
　Is that of which there's *nothing to complain*.

LINES

OCCASIONED BY A FROST IN APRIL.

  Cold, cold, my flowers!
The chill blast rudely sweeps your quivering stems,—
  Those balmy hours,
Whose breath so warmly wooed your opening gems,
  Have fled the bowers,—
And now its scythe to the destroyer lends.

  Had ye not listened to that siren tongue,
Nor spread your buds in such incautious haste,
  Ye might, ere long,
Have looked securely in the Sunbeam's face,
  And felt no wrong
Whilst gently opening in its warm embrace.

  But, fair things! thus,
In native inexperience, *your* race
  Is like to us.
We rashly give each glittering smile a place,
  And fondly nurse
The hopes which on their constancy we base,
  Till sorrows burst;
And then we find our hearts have gone to waste!

SONG.

Travelers in a world of sorrow,
　　Ye who thoughtless rove along,
Dreaming that each happier morrow
　　Will be fraught with love and song,
Let not hopes of bliss betray you;
Let not gleams of joy deceive!

Even yet while life is sweetest,
　　Ye shall find those joys decay;
And the brightest, still the fleetest,
　　Like a cloud, shall fade away.
Trust not Hope's alluring story;—
Pleasure smiles but to betray!

If the coldest bosom never
　　Found its wishes truly blest,
Why should hearts of feeling ever
　　Think to find a moment's rest?
Tenderest thoughts are soonest grievéd;
Warmest hopes are first betrayed!

But to *all*, life's troubled ocean
　　Must in bitter surges heave;
And, amid its wild commotion,
　　Ye shall many woes receive.
Think not, though your barque sail lightly,
Ye shall thus out-ride the breeze!

Travelers through a world of sorrow,
　　Roving thoughtlessly along,

SONG.

Weave not for the coming morrow
   Your bright dreams of love and song;
From delusive follies turning,
Seek the joys that ne'er deceive.

OUR BOY HEROES.

Mournful as the songs of Ossian,
  Will be "tales of other days,"
When our Southern Muse rehearses,
  In her wild and tender lays,
All the actions, and the praise
Which this bitter strife displays.

Mournful will it be, yet lovely,
  Softened in its keen regret,
When her faithful harp recalleth
  The heroic charges made,
And the oaths, so nobly kept
By her martyr sons, who slept,—

Some in crowded cemeteries,
  Some in nameless trenches thrown,
Some amid the lonely forests,
  On our shadowy hills, alone;
Or in stranger soil,— unknown,
Blanketed, without a stone!

Another yet! and yet another —
  Now the "war-path" knows no more!
Are they sleeping in their glory,
  And shall not the pæans flow
Through the ages, with the story,
How they grandly met the foe?

They from homes of ease and pleasure,
  From the halls of learning, flew,

To embrace disease and danger;
   And with loyal hearts and true,—
To the soldier's life, a stranger,
   Did the soldier's fight renew.

Tender babes, in luxury nurtured,
   Boldly faced the cannon's roar,
Boldly met the sabre charges;
   And the "red cross banner" bore
Through the serried ranks of gore
Till they fell,— to rise no more.

They, the young, the brave, the lovely,
   Precious jewels, household pets,
Hope of our dishonored land.
"Thick as leaves in Vallambrosa,"
Countless as the stars,— they met
Death in every gallant shape.

Some on their "first field" were fallen,
   Some, the heat and burden bore,—
Gnawing pains of thirst and hunger,
   Fierce alarms, and scenes of woe,
Sickening strife of blood,— before
The last act of *their* play was o'er.

Never will a wilder legend
   Follow down the ranks of time;
Never will the hoary ages
   Listen to a grander chime,—
Surging on through prose or rhyme,
Than this epic, so sublime,—

Than this sacrifice to duty,—
   Than this sacramental claim,—

This high-hearted, youthful valor,
  To preserve a home, a name,—
Than the marvel,— *how it came*,—
Striplings sprang to stalwart men

WARFARE.

"Man's a sojer; and life's a faught.'—Burns.

The world's a battle field, and he
  Who buckles on this life,
Must meet his foeman's steel, or be
  A caitiff in the strife.

Each for himself alone must stand;
  No substitute will do;
You must embattle hand to hand,
  And push it bravely through.

No armistice is ever sworn,
  No flag of truce upreared,
How-oft-soever victory's won,
  New charges are prepared.

The soldier in the ranks must fight,
  The captain at the head;
But all deserve a warrior's right,
  Who for the truth have bled.

Far down in the low vales of life
  Are men who daily strive
To battle with its wants and strife,
  And with true courage live.

Yet, he who stems temptation's flood,
  By ease and luxury raised,
Is still more soldier-like in blood,
  And no less to be praised!

Fight not to win a glorious name,
   Fight not for glittering pelf,—
The warrior who deserves most praise
   Is *conqueror of himself!*

Keep not the recompense in view,—
   The comfort for your toil;
The test of soldiership is true
   Rendition of the spoil.

Your sharpest conflicts all will end
   Just where they first begin;
The sternest tilts our trials send
   Are with indwelling sin,—

To lie in wait for evil thoughts,
   Our evil deeds control,
To check the course wrong habits brought
   And fixed upon the soul,—

To bear our daily cross with care,
   Whatever that may be,
And from our sinful hearts to tear
   Some vile idolatry.

A veteran with many scars
   Fears not the trumpet's call;
This life of warfare well prepares
   For the last joust of all.

I heard a warrior at the last
   Thus speaking to his soul:
" 'Tis done, the warfare now is past,
   And I have reached the goal.

"A good fight I have fought, henceforth
　　My weapons I lay down;
　My Judge, my righteous Judge, now doth
　　Appoint to me a crown!"

LITTLE COTTAGE HOME.

In a charming little dell where the sweetest zephyrs
        dwell,
  And the wild bees love to roam,
In joy and in content, many happy days I spent
  In my sweet little cottage home.

The red berries gleamed on the clear rippling stream,
  From the arching boughs above;
And the hawthorn pale filled with fragrance the vale
  Where our merry little footsteps roved.

But those footsteps gay have all passed away
  From that little cottage home so dear;
And of all the friends so joyous then,
  I only linger here.

SHADOWS.

"There is a skeleton in every house."

WITHIN a spacious mansion, grand and fair,
I chanced to dine. A noble pair
With stately courtesy the banquet graced,
Whose richness and profusion to the taste
Left nothing unattained. The lady's brow
Bedecked in jewels, shone with smiles just now.
My lord's reception very bland and sweet,—
When something caused by chance their eyes to meet—
A shadow crossed her face. I looked, and there,—
The skeleton behind the lady's chair!

I saw a vine-clad porch upon the street
Latticed with jasmine, and with roses sweet.
Two sisters stood behind the fragrant screen
Lovely as houri's, and more pure, I ween.
A strain of music, floating on the air,
Came stealing through the open windows there.
And then, a scream dissolved the magic spell:
A brother, reeling, on the threshold fell.
The shadow of that sorrow came before;
The skeleton had entered at the door!

One evening, unexpectedly, I went
To make a social call, where beauty lent
Attractive graces. Sisters, brothers, all,
Did honor to the old ancestral hall;
So deemed we; but with hand upon the door,
My ears were greeted by a deaf'ning roar

Of angry voices. In the stunning strife,
Each clamored, as if pleading for his life.
The shadow brooded there, with settled gloom;
The skeleton was rampant in that room!

Again, attracted by the graces sweet,
Of some fair maidens, who were wont to greet
Me, all with smiles and courtesy, I went
To tea one evening. Books and music lent
A charm to beauty. Unalloyed delight
Seemed the presiding genius of the night.
At some remark I looked up from my book,
One sister gave the other *such a look!*
The shadow vanished with a specious smile;
The skeleton grinned horribly the while!

I passed the dwelling of the man of God,—
Here he was made to pass beneath the rod,—
The gates propped up, the fences down, declare
That listlessness which springeth from despair;
The windows patched, a rose-screen hid from view,
The walls had lately sanded been, anew.
The good man's face was pinched with want, and poor,
But still his well-brushed Sunday suit he wore.
A boy came slyly out, with elbows torn;
A girl ran in, to hide her tattered gown.
I saw a meagre shadow on the floor.
The skeleton was knocking at the door!

Upon a charming friend I went to call;
They ushered me into a noble hall,
Where, garnered up, were treasuries of art,
And every luxury that could impart
A charm to wealth. A lady sweet and fair
Came in with fuschias in her braided hair.

The prattling babes climbed up upon my knee
And filled the gorgeous room with cherub glee.
"Here, then," I said, "*is happiness, at last!*"
The shadow at that moment flitted past:
A brutal speech, a sigh,— Oh, shocking race!
The skeleton was in the drunkard's face!

A pleasant message was announced one morn:
A son unto his father's house was born.
The parents sought an infant's winning ways,
But met the idiot's broad, unmeaning gaze.
I watched the boy as he grew up to man.
The little things he loved so well to scan
With driveling laughter, or with hideous rage
Denied the toys so far beneath his age.
With piteous whine he claimed his mother's love;
This, more than all things else, her pity moved.
The life-long shadow hung upon her heart,—
The skeleton could never thence depart!

A suppliant and her babe! I saw them kneel
To move a father's heart, grown hard as steel.
She had been, once, his pride and joy; but all
His hopes were crushed beneath her dreadful fall.
Unmoved by flowing tears and faded cheek,
He bade her go, some other home to seek;
And not one gleam of future hope he gave,
From infamy, his erring child to save!
She went,— the shadow took its station there.
The skeleton became that father's heir!

The millionaire lay on his couch of state,
A host of friends, assiduous, round did wait
To sooth his pain, but nothing gave him ease;
They ministered unto a mind diseased.

His only son,— long profligate and wild,—
Was now degraded by a robbery vile.
Oh, bitterest cup of all that misery brings,—
The love that's wasted on unworthy things!
"Bring pen and ink," the father said, and groaned.
'Twas brought. That son was written down disowned.
I looked around, the fatal shadow fled,—
The skeleton lay crouching on the bed!

Attracted by such screams as only come
From those long suffering in the house of doom,
I turned aside and saw a mother there,
In all the racking tortures of despair.
Her hands were manacled. That day she made
Some murderous efforts to destroy her babe.
The frightened band of children from her fly;
The husband dares not now approach too nigh.
A shadow of deep horror filled the room,—
The skeleton ran gibbering through the gloom!

I passed the quarters of the convict's cell.
There many faces were I knew full well
Had once been innocent and pure as mine,
But now were bloated and deformed by crime.
Some features still with rage and malice burned;
Some, to remorse and penitence were turned.
Their shame and misery on my pity won;
"Alas!" I said, "each was *some* mother's son!"
How many homes are shadowed o'er to-day!
How many skeletons around them play!

Oh, God of Love! Is this the state of man?
Has Nature, in reserve, no final plan
To shield him from these horrid shapes of woe
Which so torment him in this vale below?

No! While rebellions still their standards rear,
The shadows of our warfare will appear.
No rest from sin's devices may we see,
Till "Death is swallowed up in victory."
When righteousness and peace are joined in one,
The skeleton's terrific work is done.

LOVE AND THE FLOWERS.

(Under an Engraving in an Album.)

'TIS WELL he wears no brow of gloom,—
    That pretty, smiling boy,—
'Tis well no shades of sorrow come
    Across his lip of joy;
For vainly would we spread the net
    In sight of any bird;
And youthful maidens are not caught
    Where *truth* alone is heard!

Tell them "he's but a gaudy thing,
    And painted, at the best,
And that his barbed arrow stings
    To rob the heart of rest,"—
Tell them "he oftimes uses wings;
    And, though he *should* be true,
He's willful, passionate, and blind
    To every candid view,"—

Tell them "that life hath frequent scenes
    Of stern and rigid care,
For which his flatt'ries have no spell,
    His voice no fitting prayer,"—
They'll from these promptings turn away,
    As the deaf adder turns,
And bask them in the light which Love
    Upon his altar burns.

Ah, yes; he wears a wreathéd smile,
    And sports a thornless rose;

His only labor is to wile
  The heart from human woes;
He never saw a cloudy day;
  Or if some drops of rain
Did chance, he kissed them all away,
  And made things bright again!

Too sure,— too sure you are to win,
  Young mocker! in this guise;
You've scarcely any need to hold
  The mirror to her eyes;
But, lest she *see* the arrowy point,
  And dread your tyrant powers,
Take off your bow and quiver, quick
  And hide them 'neath the flowers!

MY FOREST HOME.

A QUIET spot there is, embowered in shade,
Where in my happy infancy I played;
There winter sheds a mild and genial ray,
And summer suns no arid beams display.
Tis a secluded wild. The world's rude strife
Has never breathed upon its vernal life;
Nor pride, nor pomp, nor pageantry is known
In the deep shadow of my forest home.

But skies of softest blue are beaming there,
And balmiest incense floats upon the air;
There zephyrs earliest come with laden wings,
And there the sweetest bird of summer sings.
And tints of tenderest hue and deep repose,
O'er the rich trees a veil of beauty throw
So soft and shadowy as makes life own
A dream's existence in my forest home.

A dream's existence! Aye, a poet's dream!
Where earth too Eden-like for sorrow seems,—
Where thoughts of life are blent with hallowed shades,
And sin's reality from memory fades.
Such, and so beautiful the charms, for me,
Which dwelt in that old loving forestry.—
The wildest, sweetest dreams to childhood known
Are imaged in thy shades, my forest home!

   * * * * * *

Long years of wanderings have o'er me rolled;
And other homes of love for me unfold;

Still memory, true to those embow'ring shades
Where in my happy infancy I played,—
While other scenes have on my spirit palled,--
Brings back the visions which my heart enthralled
As turns the sunflower to her god, alone
Turn I to thee, my own sweet forest home!

POOR LITTLE ZIP.

WHAT sounds that in at my casement steal,
Taking me back to the " Land o' the leal";
Where the pibroch wild the echoes fills,
As they leap from the crags on old Scotia's hills?

Run, Emmie, and Lucy, and Flossie, and Belle,—
Run, little black Pete and big black Nell;
Run one, run all, to the door and see
What this pragmatic noise can be!

There's a little brown monkey, as I'm alive!
If the three brawny showmen would but contrive
To shorten its tail, and to hide its feet,
The " metamorphose " would be complete.

His trim little jacket is dyed in red;
A jaunty cap on his little round head,
Which he snips off and on again in a trice,
And makes his " salaam " in a way quite nice.

But now the bagpipes puff and swell,
A signal that poor little Zip knows well;
So, he dances around at the length of his chain,
And snips off his little red cap again.

The children are laughing. It well may be;
For Zip has climbed to the darkey's knee,
And hangs on his back with a mawkish grin,
As much as to say, " I have found my kin!"

After this brief little escapade,
To the credit of evolution made,—
Zip mounts aloft to the arched roof,
And gives us of "natural selection" a proof.

And thus his ambition for *rising* grades
He shows, by "modification's" aid ;
But a cruel jerk, at the master's will,
Proves poor little Zip a monkey still!

The artists have placed their pipes in sheath,
To Zip's and the hearers' great relief;
A farewell nod, and his cap is doffed ;
He jumps to his seat and the band is off.

Perhaps 'tis not very wise to be
Compounding with idle vagrancy;
But "Live and let live," is a golden rule
I learned, *par cœur*, in my mother's school.

For a nickel or two and a piece of bread,
The children a merry treat have had;
If the money *is* lost, I will not cry,—
When the children are happy, so am I!

PLANTATION SKETCHES.

THE OLD HOMESTEAD.

Through the dark shadows of my later dreams
How beautiful, e'en now, to me it seems,
That grand old forest, sweeping far away
Where clouds and sunshine in the ether play,
Leaving some noble oaks to guard the dome
Of the old-fashioned house I called my home.

In the young summer's greenness, when the leaves
O'er bower and branches such a mantle weave
Of rich brocade, festooning earth and sky,
And bringing Nature's glorious mysteries nigh,
Its overpowering presence seemed to roll
A weight of beauty on my raptured soul.

And when the pale moon lighted up the night,
And, with its telegraphic fingers, strove to write,
Through the green, flick'ring draperies, on the earth,
Strange, weird thoughts within my mind had birth;
And, lingering long, I fondly watched to see
The genii peeping from each massive tree.

But, chiefly, where the hillside sloped away
Down to the east, I loved to watch the play
Of the first sunbeams as they trembling glanced
From the white maple leaves, or lightly danced
Through the notched foliage of the emerald gum,
Into a thousand silver fibers spun,—

Leaving the pea-green hickory shrubs in shade,
And, 'neath the alders, such play-houses made!

A cool, enchanting, sylvan labyrinth,
Sweet to young hearts just fresh from Nature's mint,
With golden sassafras in pleasant view,
Delicious red-bud, and the honey dew—

Dotting the long leaves of the grand papaw
Where humming-birds their sweetest nectar draw
From amber blossoms in rich clusters spread;
And, singing at their work, high overhead,
The cheerful bees with music filled the air
Already redolent with perfume, where —

Prolific bullaces and flowering grape
Enwreathed the boughs in every graceful shape.
Were ever trees like these? Or does the grand
Old earth afford a spot so exquisitely plann'd
As that which first, upon our dawning eyes,
As home, sweet home, broke in its glad surprise?

As mem'ry to the mirrored haunts of youth
Carries me back, the old paths lie before me in their truth,
Fresh as if yesterday they guided me
To scenes enchanting in their novelty.
Years vanish,— and the interlude of pain,—
I seem to be a happy child again!

Upon the loving portal now I stand,
But not alone. With me a merry band
As e'er plucked berries from the topmost bough,
And mastered obstacles,— no matter how,—
Three noble boys, discursive, active, wild,
Sportive as lambs, and just as free from guile.

The fairest blossoms of the woods they knew;
And who, so well as they, where wild plums grew?

The earliest nuts their secret treasuries filled;
They dammed the brook to work our mimic mill,
Or launched our tiny boats upon the stream
Where the deep water looked so still and green.

We drank from leaf-cups at the crystal spring;
And to old gnarled roots did mosses bring
Richer than Brussels; and our shelves we filled
With acorn cups,— in sage housewif'ry skilled,—
Played out our little parts upon that stage,
The mimic Buskins of a future age!

Oh, blessed age! and blessed infancy!
Which may to Nature's charms devoted be,
At ease to con her lessons o'er,
And every nook and cairn of hers explore;
Imbibing healthful air and germs of taste,
Stored up against the days of fashion's waste;

Strengthening the soul against the power of sin;
Keeping all pure and bright and fresh within;
Kindling a glow that never can grow cold;
Training a heart that never will grow old;
Making all life a holiday to see;
A gala robe of every bush and tree!

Alas! for those cribb'd in malarial rooms,
Or mid the city's vice-surrounded glooms!
Old in their infancy with dearth and care,
The creature's wants no generous motives share!
How sad to have no leisure to begin
Life with the birds, and Nature's blessings win!

Benevolence and Joy go hand in hand;
This, we were early taught to understand,

And soon the happy almoners became
Of one, who, though she never heard the voice of Fame.
Wears yet a crown in heaven! Angel of mercy, she
The poor sought out, without partiality.

One of the foot-ways that we loved to tread,
Down by the "quarters" huts and gardens, led
Along the hillside through a copse of pines,
And stopped upon the marshy, damp confines
Of a small streamlet. Here, at fall of eve
The tribes of "Rana" would their concert weave,—

The doleful hootings of the owl were heard,
The bat's sharp cry, the beetle's angry "thud,"
And all the dismal voices of the wood.
But on this dreary spot a dwelling stood;
Homely and small, yet rudely circled round
With some artistic rows of garden ground.

Cabbage and onions there had found a place,
And that "vile weed," suggestive of a race
Excitable. What lured to this uninviting spot
The merry children of a happier lot?
Errands of love, which every tyro knows
Can make the desert blossom with the rose!

"Old Agathie" lured there! A lonely being she,
Who, in mistaken kindness was set free,
A pensioner upon the world's great debt,
With none to press her claim, and yet
She had her freedom,—yes, but nothing else;
The "Cup of Tantalus" was all her wealth!

A long probation God had given her then,
And so she felt,—poor Agathie!—as when

With modest mien she wandered up and down,
Where no relief, no sympathy was found;
And wondered why she could not cast the shell
Of old mortality, and with the angels dwell.

To want no more! And yet, she murmured not,
But met with quiet dignity her lot;
Accepting for her yarn, or knitted stuff,
Scant courtesy sometimes, and oft rebuff;
Still trusting wholly in his word who said,
The righteous never shall be wanting bread.

At length that God who hears the raven's call,
And notes the tiny sparrows when they fall,
Her weary feet to the " Old Homestead " brought,
Where quickly rose for her the humble cot.
To that good Master's generous ear and brain
The appeal of woman ne'er was made in vain!

"Curses come home to roost," then why not say
Blessings their donors amply will repay,
Even as the sun-drawn vapors fall again,
Refreshing earth with gentle dews and rain?
Just so the Lord that household well repaid
For deeds of mercy to his dark handmaid.

Unpolished, ignorant she must have been,
Despised by many for her ebon skin.
But love of holy things had schooled her sense
Above the worldling's merely vain pretence;
The strong desire to know the word of God,
A keener culture gave than rule or rod.

What most we love, in that we best succeed;
Enthusiasm is "God in us," indeed!

The Christian's thoughts, however weak or great,
From contemplating God, will imitate;
Thus prayer ennobles and refines the thought,
And brings reflection,— in the schools untaught.

This mental training in her manner fused
A conciousness of worth, with modest use.
Of all the forms which to her state belonged,
She neither servant nor master wronged,
And thus in her serene and quiet way,
She set a meek example, day by day.

But not content with this, she oft bestowed
Drops from the pious fountain, which o'erflowed
Her loving heart, to all who kindness gave;
And much she strove her countrymen to save!
Yet, the great " Pearl of price " would recommend
To her superiors who an ear would lend.

Most precious now, among the things that be,
An olden picture, which I often see
In mem'ry's necromantic glass,— a sweet
And youthful mother on a cushioned seat,
A dark-browed woman, with her eyes of greed,
Intent upon the " Word of Life " to feed.

That mother, mid the freshest joys of life,
The loving parent, and the model wife,
Had yet, perhaps, no soberer thoughts embraced;
But who shall say, that in her after race,
She did not with this blessed truth agree:
" Who water others, they shall watered be "?

THE PIONEER.

I.

Oh, Time and Sorrow! Hallowed is the touch
   Ye give the past! Soft as the mother's tread
Beside the sleeping babe; even such
   Is the kind hand with which ye raise the dead
From the dark sleep of years, while all too much
   Our hearts are weeping for the voices fled;
And joys come limping on their broken crutch,
   Most faithfully and sadly by you led
   Down the long vista, opening still and dread!

II.

No mirth irrever'nt, nor mocking spleen,
   Vented on "other days" can ye endure;
No censures harsh, nor ridicule profane,
   Dare touch the beauty of the "things of yore";
Ye have the secret sign, the true "sesame,"
   To all the dearest things life hath in store;
And vulgar footsteps ne'er shall enter in
   That sacred portal, locked by you before
   The aroma of life was breathed no more.

III.

Its perfumed cloisters open then to me,
   And from the many portraits hung upon
Its walls, the dust brush off, that I may see
   The dark, yet pleasant lineaments of one,
Who, though imperfect, gave to you and me
   Our due unasked, and then, his duty done,
Went up, in heaven a servitor to be.

Let not the tall, gaunt form provoke to fun,
Nor the crisp, hoary locks the finic stun;

IV.

For beauty does not live in form or eye,
    Nor in the *toute ensemble*. On the whole,
'Tis the electric flash,— the pure psychology,
    The intact of one intellectual soul
With kindred essences, by which the high
    And nobler impulses, which o'er us roll,
Strike off some sparks from immortality!
    No stoics are ye, of the olden school,
    Seeking perfection by the cynics' rule.

V.

The veil of charity then softly throw,
    In hazy shadowings, o'er the frailties found
In the poor dwellers on this vale below.
    The rougher angles gently softened down
Bring back the generous traits which did abound
    In my old friend; the delicate perceptions shown,
The courtesy, which threw such grace around
    His deeds, and we shall see the *personnel*
    The mere *exterieure* very far excel!

VI.

The "Old Plantation's" sturdy pioneer,—
    His strong arm fashioned the first rustic "bield,"
His good arm trained the earliest furrows there;
    "How jocund did he drive his team afield"
To gather in the yellow grain with care,
    Or, for the semi-annual jaunt to market, yield
His most sagacious ken. This *chef d'œvre*
    Was looked upon with no small interest where
    His safe return was crowned with so much cheer.

VII.

Beside the "good things," stored for household use,
  Brave, thrifty "Jim" from his own crop could spare
Nuts for the "wee ones" of his master's house,
  And "lots" of fineries for his daughters dear,
And by his dealing with a hand so loose
  He came the reputable name to bear
Of "Uncle Jim," the richest, and, in truth,
  Most generous of colored gentlemen, so near
  Does thrift the garb of real virtue wear!

VIII.

His mental calibre and taste were far
  Above the herd; but, more than this, he stood
A prince among his class. In peace and war,
  Un homme galant he was, both brave and good!
Few stronger arms, or kinder hearts there are!
  And none to aid the weak more promptly would;
But better yet than this, he kept a cow,
  A score of "hives," fruit trees and herbs; and sure
  His place as "Host" was then no sinecure!

IX.

Moreover, he his visitors could while,
  Of many a vacant hour, with "tales of old,"
Told in his own unique and racy style,—
  Of revolutionary days, grown bold
In crime, unlicensed. Oft he won a smile
  With cunning tricks of hand he did unfold.
Trained early by a master brave but wild,
  By which the "traitor's" noblest steeds he stole,
  Though yet a simple waiter — ten years old!

X.

Some small obliquities of speech and eye,
  ~ Gained in this evil school, "finesse," in short.

Joined to his manner bland, and piety,
  Made union so grotesque, that in some sort
His name did under imputations lie.
  Unlike great Cæsar's wife, he was not thought
Above suspicion of — hypocrisy!
  How many a charge, by prejudices wrought,
  Dissolves when to the sun of truth 'tis brought.

XI.

When, as a curious child, I often sought
  The kitchen walk, seated upon his knee,
I listened to his loving words about
  The Master, Jesus. Afterward, when free
To wander as I listed, oft my route
  Inquisitive would through his garden be,
Or near the windows of his hives, to see
  The working bees go softly in and out,
  Peering most curiously where I should not.

XII.

Then gently would he stop my roving feet,
  And point me to that blest but narrow way
Which only enters at the heavenly gate,
  And where the only watchword is, to pray;
Or, shuddering, warn me of that broad, broad street,
  Down which, in visions, both by night and day,
He saw the thousands rushing on to meet,
  In mad succession, all the woes that lie
  In the dread chasm of eternity!

XIII.

My poor old friend this testimony hath
  To his sincerity: The Saviour saith
Of him that's sheltered from the coming wrath,
  "The left hand knows not what the other doth."
His love for souls was witness to his faith;

And, though his early life had been but rough,
His last days were his best.   His evening path
  Was like the blessed pathway of the just,
  Which shineth more and brighter than at first.

XIV.

Long has he been upon that blissful shore,
  Which, with the eye of faith, he long had seen,
Where tempests never beat nor billows roar.
  Though vigorous with his four-score years and ten,
He had been daily looking heavenward more,
  Waiting the coming of the Son of Man.
At last, he laid him down, the journey o'er,
"As one who wraps the drapery of his couch
  About him, and lies down to pleasant dreams."

XV.

It is a blessed thought, old friend, that here,
  Living for others, you were taught to die!
That cleansing Fountain, ever fresh and pure,—
  But in your own bright land, so parched and dry,—
Gushed from the Word of Life, and followed near
  Your toil-worn steps, and lightened every sigh,
And made the paths of duty easier.
  Light work it was to purchase glory's crown
  By a few years of privilege laid down!

POOR RACHEL.

I.

As DOWN through the valley of sorrow I passed,
Pursuing the pleasures too fleeting to last,
Near the home of my childhood I found me once more;
But, alas! for the things so delightful before;
The beautiful forest, the joy of my youth,
Had fallen a prey to utility's ruth.

II.

Of all the grand oaks which the genii had claimed,
One relic, one beautiful relic, remained;
The vandal had driven the cruel plow-share
Through all my gay circles and flow'ry *parterre;*
The old faded house, where my parents had died,
And where I had lived as their joy and their pride,—

III.

Towered dark and defiant; from every closed door
The requiem sounded, "No more! never more!"
The windows deserted, where once I had seen
So many young faces the shutters between,
Looked down on me sadly and silently there,—
I felt cold and benumbed in my gloomy despair!

IV.

But as in my ramblings I stopped at the door
Of a little old cabin, most wretchedly poor,
Whence the soul of a servant ascended above,
The iceberg dissolved, and my heart was so moved

With the thought of her patient devotion for years,
That my stubborn rebellion was melted to tears.

V.

Perhaps 'twas a feeling connected with shame,
Or something akin to a self-adjudged blame,
Recalling a sense of her meekness and worth,
And the small share of comfort she had upon earth;
But 'twas thy last lesson, poor Rachel, to show
That out of thy ashes one blossom could grow,—

VI.

The blossom of pity,— remembering her look
So quiet and peaceful, which nothing e'er shook!
Like Anna, long years she a widow had been;
Like Anna, she walked by the Prompter within;
And her faith in the Saviour as ardently burned
As in those to the Temple who constantly turned.

VII.

Few aids did she have in her strife to be good,
Poor Rachel! but always she did what she could.
"I think," said her mistress, "if Rachel had found
A pin, she would seek for the owner around."
By all who best knew, this witness was borne:
No wrong done by Rachel had ever been known.

VIII.

With that blessed old mistress, whose life was all praise,
Poor Rachel had lived in her happier days!
But the fierce bolts of Time the old roof-tree had riven,
And mistress and follower for shelter were driven
Beneath the kind homestead, where, past things forgot,
She meekly took up and accepted her lot.

IX.

No wonder she pitied the desolate lamb!
How often, in passing, I came to a stand,
And exchanged a soft smile, as with one hand she fed
And the other around it caressingly laid.
Though Rachel was black and the lamb was snow white
They seemed to me, always, most strikingly 'like!

X.

Poor Rachel! I mind me *one* failing she had,
In the eyes of the gourmand esteemed very bad;
For when, as it chanced, she *cuisiniere* did play,
The children were likely to call it "fast day."
"What a sin," she would murmur, "to eat like a goose,
When things might be laid up for somebody's use."

XI.

One *failing*, but then she had charity, large,
And virtues sufficient to cover this charge.
Ever gentle, and thoughtful of others' complaints,
With a heart overflowing in love to the saints,
She mourned over all under Satan's control,
And gave her small mite to the conquest of souls,—

XII.

The mite of her influence. When morning had come,
She oft made excuses to enter my room,
And kneeling, would round me her faithful arms wrap,
And resting a moment her head on my lap,
Would anxiously ask what I found on the page,
And what were the musings in which I engaged.

XIII.

And then she would point to the Fountain of Love,
And urge me to place my affections above.

But in her pure mind still there lingered a doubt,
If as Christians we left the poor colored race out.
Assured the reverse, her scruples all fled,
She received me as one just awaked from the dead.

XIV.

Changes came o'er me with years. I'd become
Guest rather than inmate of that cherish'd home;
But in every reunion no welcome there beamed
More brightly than Rachel's. One day I deemed
Some mischief befallen. They whispered me low,—
A long journey she was preparing to go.

XV.

The Master had called her, and glad she obeyed,
And now in the fair land of "Beulah" she strayed,
With the mountains "Delectable" full in her view,
As nearing the gates of the city she drew.
For weeks on the banks of the river she lay,
Then joyous, like Hopeful, she passed o'er the way.

XVI.

Poor Rachel! the waters her feet came not near,
As she left the poor cabin for the mansion fair,
And she heard on the border the sweet welcoming
For those who in few things so faithful have been;
But much shall I wonder if in her bright crown,
Some stars,— to her modest surprise,— are not found.

OLD GEOFFREY.

That face was in itself a picture! peaceful, pure,
   For more than twenty years it was as now,
Save that the grizzled hair still whiter grew,
   And thinner, on the high and polished brow.
Why should it change? He shared the golden mean
From luxury to poverty between;
His head was sheltered from the storms of care,
Want had no power to place its fingers there.

His voice was always very low and soft,
   His manner ever courteous and serene,
And from his meek address I've looked up oft
   To mark the selfish cunning which is seen
Under a servile mask, but found, the while,
The truthful candor of a little child.
Why should he fawn, or crouch, all men before?
His heritage was safe, his bread and water sure.

No! let the vassal crook the supple knee,
   And cater for the fee his lordling grants;
No need of canvassing was here, and he
   Can well afford to bow who nothing wants.
Deep in the law of universal love
Old Geoffrey's code was laid, and thus it proves,
Whatever may be said of race or clan,
Nature and grace do form the gentleman!

How pleasantly it loometh up to view,
   That kind old face of bright mahogany,
Content and thankful, smiling and yet true,

The poet's paragon of honesty!
The study of that face were better far
Than all the scientists' unmeaning war,
To show,— whatever epiderms they wear,—
All men some traces of God's image bear.

For half a century, the good old man!
   The happiest osculations of his star
Round the old homestead in conjunction ran
   With some dark planet, daily circling there.
True to the claims and instincts of his race,
No "visit-evening" missed him from his place,
Where the "auld gude wife" ever had in store
Small share of "'plenishin'," but kindness more.

The Scottish bard has very wisely taught,
   In happiness there's no monopoly;
Those sable children of a lowly lot
   Envied no prince his higher destiny.
The human heart has only one great want,
Content the only riches God doth grant;
To this their simple habitudes drew near,
Which home and homely comforts more endear.

If joys were few, so also were their cares;
   No dreams of rental, or a landlord's frown,
Harrowed the hours of rest, nor did the fears
   Of tax on bread make it go harshly down.
The merry laugh of comfort was not stilled
By dread forebodings of the sexton's bill,—
Happiest of all the poor! The Golden Age
Seemed coming back in their blest pupilage!

Ambition's fevered dream disturbed them not,
   Nor love of money won their souls from heaven;

But world forgetting, by the world forgot,
    Their thoughts to pure devotion could be given.
Such was the humble pair, who child-like drew
Their wants from others, and who never knew
Nor anxious thoughts nor frowns, but in their
    place
They lived together as the heirs of grace,—

And made the cot a bethel. Oft at eve,
    When o'er the dwelling hung some trembling
        star,
I, with my playmates, daring scarce to breathe,
    Gave audience to that unpresuming prayer;
No precedent my early years had known,
How strangely sounded then that monotone,
Which, like the bread that's gathered up again
After a length of days,— through all the din—

Of busy, troublous years has sweetly grown
    A *sotto voce* on my heart, recalling truth
Which comes to innocence, and that alone.
    When wearied with religious forms, forsooth,
When sick of falsehoods and the hollow sound
Of tinkling cymbals, which so much abound,
To me that simple, self-forgetting prayer
Is what to drooping flowers the dewdrops are!

The purest hearts most credulous are found.
    Poor Geoffrey innocently thought that he,
In lines which in the human hand abound,
    The path of life for every one could see!
How vainly, then, I tried to reconcile
This fortune-telling with his want of guile.
Experience since has shown that all men have
Some crotchets of the brain, which idly rave!

OLD GEOFFREY.

Methinks I see him, as I saw him stand
   One holiday, in modest attitude,
Bending above the delicate, soft hand
   Of a capricious damsel, fair but rude;
The many crosses interwoven there
O'ercame the courtesy of the old seer;
No answer to her anxious quest he gave,
Except a boding shake of his sage head.

Science he knew not, nor had heard the name
   Of palmistry. Relic of heathen art,
Transmitted through the æons, down it came
   To poor old Geoffrey, who received, in part
From sheer tradition, from experience more,
In all the sequences which daily flow
From outward causes, and the fruitful train
Of ideas from temperament and manner gained.

Time rolled apace. His faithful partner died;
   But the old prophet lingered still around
The pleasant scene, where, in his manhood's pride,
   So much of true contentment he had found.
The path, long trod, had worn into his heart;
His feet refused to trace another part.
Again the matrimonial bond he framed, and then
The family altar builded up again.

Again he was bereaved; and yet,
   Leaning upon the staff of four-score years,
The even tenor of his way he kept,
   Unmoved by dark regrets, or bitter fears,
And still his face shone with a soft delight,
As one who in reserve has treasures bright
Beyond the reach of casualties,— joys
Which nothing earthly gives nor yet destroys.

At length the paths were silent, which before
   The old man trod. He came no more abroad.
Doubtless 'twas comfortless and very poor
   Where now he lay,— that widow'd abode,—
To other eyes; but so illumined by
A Saviour's love, a palace seemed it nigh
To him, cheered, too, by kind attentions done,
Which years of faultless servitude had won.

No riches, but that blessed faith he had;
   No warrior qualities to win renown,
But the most obdurate of all things bad,
   The human heart, he won. They who had known
Benevolence for none now dealt as mild
And tenderly with him as with a child.
And thus he passed away, obscure, unknown,
But calendared by him, the three in one,
" Who sees with equal eye, as God of all,
A hero perish, or a sparrow fall."

THE BROKEN HEART.

Thou brightly flowing river! in thy green
And wide savannahs, many a pleasant scene
Lies 'neath the hills, nestling, as doth the babe,
In loving arms, shut in from the parade
And glare of fashion, and the rude alarms
Which flow from social contact and its harms.

'Twas thus, at least, when Peace and Plenty reigned,
Or ere Suspicion's foul and bloody train
Had entered these sweet Edens of delight,
And o'er the bowers spread a moral blight;
Or ere Contentment, sweetest charm of earth,
Was driven from the home where she had birth.

Some of these homesteads yet, as pictures fair,
Daguerrotyped upon my mem'ry are.
The sun which gilded them hath darkly set,
The beauty fled, but I can ne'er forget
Sweet C———, the glowing landscape which once spread
Its soft enchantment round my youthful head.

The lordly mansion, standing in its prime,
Bore witness to a soft and happy clime;
The doors and windows, amply large and tall,
Let in a flood of light upon the hall,
Which, faced on either side by porches high,
Took in the breezes and cerulean sky.

From that grand porch which fronted on the west,
An ample terrace reached the open space,
Whence you might gain a comprehensive view
Of features ever bright and ever new:
The winding river, the fair azure hills
Of Georgia, the intervening acres tilled,—

Broad acres, varied with the grazing flocks
And cheerful husbandmen, who sorrow mocked.
The south view added to the scene around
The more inspiring symphonies of sound;
The soft, sweet cooings of the pigeon-cote;
The tinkle of the sheep-bell on the slope;—

The "click-clack" where the blacksmith's hammer fell;
The whirling of the pulley at the well;
The playful children, with their merry chimes;
The soughing of the wind among the pines;
And sometimes, over all these mingling came,
Harmoniously, a clear, commanding strain,—

Sonorous as a silver trumpet's call,
When something bright and cheery doth befall.
'Tis truth to say, that, to my childish ear,
That sound had more of comfort and good cheer
Than any music I have ever heard
While traveling since along a pathway weird.

That sound, so silvery and stirring, came
From good "Aunt Cassie," *chef de la cuisine*,
Transporting me into the basement clean,
Upon whose floor no stain was ever seen,
And where the snowy table was set out
With viands of the most exquisite art.

THE BROKEN HEART.

From the long corridor, some breezy morn,
You might look down upon her stately form,
In striped homespun clad and 'kerchief clean,
The sable empress of a wide domain!
Busied with dishes "done just to a charm;"
Or, sleeves rolled up above her dimpled arm.

In the cool morning or the fervid noon,
Adjusting with much care the bib and spoon
For some one of the little cherubs fair,
With faces round, and long, black, silky hair,
Who, ever pulling at her apron strings,
Had twined themselves around her heart's best
    springs.

Her selfish interests she had outlived far,—
If that, indeed, there had been any there;—
Her hours of relaxation all were given
To these, her only children this side heaven;
And though the offshoots of that thriving tree
Beneath whose shade she dwelt so pleasantly,—

Numbered, at length, nine, ten, or even more,
Her face was still as lustrous as before;
Still, on the nice brick pavement, morn and noon,
With patient joy wielding the bib and spoon,
Her loving care was just as fresh and warm
As when one fairy nestled on her arm.

*   *   *   *   *   *   *

A change fell rudely on that lovely scene,—
Sudden and fearful had the onset been,
As some dark cloud, which rises in the west,
While still serene and smiling is the rest
Of heaven's frontispiece, and, ere we know
That danger threatens, stuns us with the blow.

So came misfortune's tempest, laying low
The verdant hopes, and turning into woe
Thoughts which had slept on velvet until now,
And rose-hued visions which from pleasure grow.
The besom of destruction was complete,
Swept every comfort was from 'neath their feet!

The cheerful hands, the lowing herds, away
Were taken, the insolvent's debt to pay.
The cooings from the pigeon-cote alone
Responded to that melancholy moan,
When she, the foster-mother, friend, and cook,
Turned from her new captivity to look,—

For the last time upon that cherish'd spot,
Where, all the slave's sad destiny forgot,
She tasted pleasures such as rarely fall
To those who do themselves the honored call.
Oh! who shall tell her anguish and dismay,
As from her airy realm she turned away,—

And children of her love! to try anew
The stranger paths, and stranger faces, too?
They placed her, rudely, in another home,
Nor once bethought them how she loved her own.
Only one little month had sadly fled;
One morn they tried to wake, and found her—dead!

THE IGNIS FATUUS, OR GONDEMA AND FABRICIO.

W. C. M.

'Twas in the darkness of an autumn night;
  The black o'erhanging clouds had quite shut out
Fair Luna and the glimmering starlight;
  The deep-toned, sullen thunder rolled along,
  The vivid lightning, flashing swift and strong,
Illumed the deep, dark vale through which the route
Of Gondema must lead, as half in doubt
  And half in trust she issued from the hut
Where "brethren" met at duty's call, to pray;
  So much reliance in these prayers she put,
No boding cloud could frighten her away;
  The rain, which long in torrents rattling fell,
  On the new-fallen leaves, like clumps of hail
Upon the housetops, now dissolved in mist;
  When Gondema the blind path wended slow
  That to her cottage led. Years four score
Made up her sum of days. Now gray with age
  Her hair, its native kink in curl displayed
'Neath her white cap. Old Time had waged
  War with her dusky brow, but left it this
Impress of humble peace: a look that's undismayed.

Adown the slippery hill her careful steps
  One of the "faithful" held. On her return,
Where two ways met, her light went out. She kept
  Courageously her course toward the bourn
Of mighty rest. The mist began more heavily to drip,
  The thunder through the hollows grumbled loud,

And as the zigzag lightning danced and skipped
  Across her path, it gradually made known
The fearful truth which conjured up a crowd
  Of superstitious fancies — she was lost!
In the dark windings of the dismal swamp
  No way-marks now her feeble eyes accost.
Trembling with panic-fear, and chilled with damp,
  Oft she essayed her aged voice to raise,
  To invoke his aid who through so many days
  Of lonely widowhood had given her light,
  And "songs had given her" in the dreary night;
But naught these pious turns of thought availed.
  The fiend had rolled her senses like a scroll,
Her tongue was knotted, and despair assailed
  The heart that had so many pulses told
Of truth unfaltering.   Fixed she stood, as in a reverie
     deep,
When lo! through the deep fearful copse a taper peeped
  Lurid and ghastly, but with stealthy stride
  Seemed moving on.   Low did it glide,
As seeking through the mold
  Sure footing for the traveler's weary feet.
  So thought poor Gondema!   That light to greet
She started with an anxious shout, and fell
  With palsied haste into a marshy fen.
  Alas! how many, far more wise, have been
Duped by a light which promised quite as well,
  Yet proved at last to be no light from heaven,
  But miasmatic gleams by error driven.
Recovering soon, but not her wonted pace,
Old Gondema looked up her way to trace;
  Her light was gone.   No! yonder, flick'ring through
  The bending willows, it is still in view!
With all the speed that she could now essay,
  Through the stiff, reedy bog, o'er rushes high,
  In itoloniferous roots entangled nigh,

Sinking in pools and mire, she made her way
   Led by Supernal power, for that alone
   Supported her, and by this spell drawn on,
   Though weak with age, and nearly dead with fright,.
   She followed eagerly that phantom light,
Till waning to a speck it died away
   Into the murky midnight. Farther on
   Again it glowed. Poor Gondema, forlorn
   And crazed, plunged through the winding stream,
   And grievously entranced by that gleam
Sank down exhaustedly, her tresses gray
   Loaded with vapors, and her garments torn
With thorns and briars. From the adjacent hill
   Her cry for help was piteously borne
Through the conducting air, now moist and still,
   To where the "brethren" yet their vigils kept,
And reached Fabricio's ears, that aged friend
Whose gallant arm, raised ever to defend
   A sister's cause, had not been palsied yet!

"Hist!" cried he, "heard I not afar some doleful sound,.
Like one in agony of trouble found?
It seems that from the summit of yon hill
It comes,— some one is farin' ill!"
More faint, yet dolefuler the sound appeared.
"Did I not tell you so? 'Tis sister Gondema, misled
   By Jack o' Lantern." This having said,
   The brave old man stayed not to marshal fears,
   But, turning his *old hat the inside out*,
   He seized his torch and bounded through the night,.
Like a dim meteor in the heavens. His route
   Directly o'er the rugged hillside lay;
   And leaping over all that checked his way,
Huge roots and rocks, and, frightful to the sight,
Great fissures that laid open to the light
   The secrets of the earth, which science owed

To gravitating waters in their flood,
He paused and made survey with anxious eye,
But nothing, in the darkness, could espy.
He raised his lusty voice: "Gondema! Gondema!"
  The hills reverberate the cheerful sound,
The trembling echoes whispered back, "ema."
  Then all was still, except a feeble voice,
And as the sable champion looked around,
  He saw the victim and her airy guide.
The spell was now resumed, that had been lost
  Just for a time. With tottering step she tried
The charm to follow still. Upon her knees
  She fell, with trace scarce visible of life;
Endangered seemed the last Promethean spark;
Again she rose, and stumbling through the dark,
  Pursued the author of her night of strife;
But in a moment more, the spell, with ease,
  Fabricio broke. He took the hat from off his hoary head,
  And, as a bubble bursts, the phantom fled!

"He is a freeman whom the truth makes free!"
Reader, the chains of superstition see,
More deadly, sure, than those which wear the flesh.
The demon of the swamp, the vile "fetish,"
The good and evil days, the serpent charms,
The "rider of the broomstick" which alarms
  The sleep of all who take not care to nail
A horse-shoe at the door, and on whose shrine
  Thousands must yearly bleed in lands which hail
The black man's sires! What truths sublime
Come down, transfigured by the touch of Time,
From ages past! Error has flown away
Before the dawning of the promised day.
To those who sat in heathen gloom at home,
No matter how delivered, *light has come!*

www.ingramcontent.com/pod-product-compliance
Lightning Source LLC
Chambersburg PA
CBHW020310170426
43202CB00008B/561